THE TRUE STORY OF BRITTANY MOSER

FREE AND FEARLESS

The Amazing Impact of One Precious Life

Michael,

Live for your adventure!

Phil Moser

Praise for *Free and Fearless*

In his book, *Free and Fearless,* Philip Moser gives readers a glimpse into his cherished relationship with his daughter, Brittany, throughout her life, through blissful and difficult times. But more so, he communicates how he has been able to find that life after death is not an end, but a new and still hopeful beginning, and how Brittany has taught him and his family that she is strongest with them when they are making peace with the past and pursuing the freedom that the joys of living fearlessly and graciously can bring. Even though death leaves a sting, a life lived well will never really die. Brittany Moser was a blazing soul that burned passion for life into those she encountered, and she continues to do so.

Rachael Barry-Former
Hamilton News Reporter

When reading a book like this you pause many times over the words. Metamorphosis, because it's a true story of how a family morphed together and brought others along for the adventure. A change happened in each life the Moser's encountered. Being "Grounded in Gratitude" that our chrysalis has broken, and we can spread our wings and be touched by the love, courage, and soul of these wonderful people. We ask permission to gaze with you at "rainbow dust" and know you as friends!

John and Christine Odle
author

Free and Fearless touched my soul on so many levels. This remarkable and enchanting story about a Free and Fearless warrior woman teaches us of love, unconditionally love and devotion written through the eyes of a father.

Jenny Sutton-Godsey

The **internet and social media** have made the world much more transparent. Negative news about chiropractors, sadly, causes many people to not walk through a chiropractor's doors. As the saying goes: *Do something right and a patient will tell two people. Do something wrong and they will tell everyone they know.*

If all this isn't enough there is something else going on: The **decrease in the relative value** of a chiropractic office visit.

Potential patient says: *Why pay $50 for a 10-minute chiropractic visit when I can pay the same amount and get an entire month's worth of a fitness class that is more enjoyable?*

Potential patient says: *Why would I pay $40 for a 10-minute chiropractic visit when I can get a full hour massage for $60?*

No amount of "chiropractic education" can change this mindset. Of course, working out can never do what chiropractic can. Massage can never do what chiropractic can, but that is not what is important. What is important is how much money the typical health consumer is willing to pay for a chiropractic office visit.

The perfect storm: Nobody knows what a chiropractor does any more. There is a chiropractor on every corner, loads of negative information online, chiropractors cheapening the profession to embarrassing levels, insurance companies making you do paperwork and sit on hold for 20 minutes only to not pay you anything, downward economic pressure, huge debt that is almost insurmountable, the cost of everything from cars to houses has skyrocketed, people have more choices than ever, and people who would rather pay for a quick-fix-feel-good thing vs. long term care to actually repair a problem.

This is the reason I moved out of the building I owned. I even sold the building as the overhead ratio would never work with chiropractic, the economy, and insurance companies were headed.

I realized that a chiropractic business has to be modeled after hard market facts, NOT on irrelevant or emotional personal beliefs.

The good news is, you can profit from this! Despite the storm of turbulence in chiropractic, a successful career is still possible! The best way is with the low overhead, high production, high value, high fun, and the superior money flow model that only we have!

Our Chiropractic Success Program

The goal is simple: To make you the most successful chiropractor that your God given ability will allow. Another goal I have for you is to become the most successful chiropractor who ever lived in your area!

I can say with passion that being a successful chiropractor is something that I love. WINNERSEDGE principles are how I have done it. You can do it too! You simply have to say: *I am going to do it!*

Now I am not saying you should join WINNERSEDGE, what I am saying is, when you join a high-performance chiropractic consulting group your success can be greatly accelerated.

It feels great to know you have the information and resources you need to handle all aspects of practice start-up and growth. It feels even better to be a winner! *With us, that is what we are here to do!*

- Do you want to have an office that you and your patients **love**?
- Do you want to become a master at running your own practice?
- Do you want to know how to fill the place with great patients?
- Do you want to know how to pay off every penny of your loans?
- Do you want to know how to **collect more** than you thought?
- Do you want to become an expert with your business skills?
- Do you want to learn how to become a **money handling master**?
- Do you want to avoid the endless landmines that catch most DCs?
- Do you want to **become a millionaire** from giving your service?
- Do you want to be friends with super successful chiropractors?
- Do you want to see amazing places and do amazing things?
- Do you want your relationship life to reach another level?
- Do you like the idea of only working 24 hours a week?
- Do you want low stress and high **fun in practice**?

Calls

- I do a one-hour video *Zoom* call every month for DCs and CAs!
- You can also have private training calls with me directly.
- All member DCs and CAs can call or email me <u>personally</u> anytime. My accessibility is what makes WE unique.

Website

- You get passcodes to our **video library** where we have over 500 practice success videos on everything you want to know!
- Here you can download our incredible **12 Phase Practice Transformation Guide**. It works, believe me!
- You can also access all recorded and archived *Zoom* training calls.
- All Seminars are made into a 30-min synopsis video and includes our Seminar Booklet for those unable to attend.
- You get our invaluable list of WINNERSEDGE contacts for: Websites, equipment, experts, marketing, everything.

Events

- 5 **True Chiro Success Seminars** each year for all DCs, spouses and staff. All member DCs have a nametag waiting for them.
- Access to all **Workshops** and our legendary **BOOTCAMPS**.
- I also offer private trainings in your office or in my own office!

And

- WINNERSEDGE Toolkit: Practice, Business and CA Essentials plus Bonus materials are sent to all members ASAP.
- DCs and CAs also each have their own WE Facebook group.

Whether you are starting from scratch, wanting to double an existing practice, or looking for a smart retirement strategy, **call us.**

Learn more about the incredible WINNERSEDGE *Mach1* high-performance chiropractor coaching program, simply call or contact us at winnersedgeconsulting.com.

I wish you the best of luck, success, and happiness in all your chiropractic endeavors. I hope you join us so you too can **become a chiropractic warrior!**

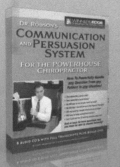

A loving story of a father's devotion to his daughter. From great heartache to an inspirational journey.

Katie Heaton
Mississippi Valley Library District

Phil and Brittany's story is so unique. He's taken what could have been life-altering in the worst way and made it into something truly heartwarming. Most people would take a tragedy like he experienced and wallow in the grief, but not Phil, because that's not what Brittany would have wanted. Full of Brittany magic, *Free and Fearless* is a true story that shows not only the unending love and devotion between a father and his daughter but also one man and his family's passion to live as Brittany wanted them to.

Ashlee Hoos
The Herald-Republican newspaper, KPC Media Group

A truly inspiring story that reminds you about the important things in life.

Rex Smith
Broadcaster

Free and Fearless tells the story of a daughter and her dad, and how her life-taking illness has helped him discover that each day is a joy.

A father, faced with the most difficult challenge in his life, losing his daughter, sets out on a bucket list of journeys. Along the way, he meets strangers who want to share Brittany's story of determination, love of life, and love of family.

Andy St. John
WLKI FM100.3 radio personality

By telling Brittany's story and completing her bucket list, Phil channeled his grief into a fulfilling journey. He hopes this will provide comfort for others who have lost a child.

Pat Waters

FREE AND FEARLESS

The Amazing Impact of One Precious Life

PHIL MOSER

Edited by Sandy Redden and Dale Dailey
Cover and Book Design by James Woosley (FreeAgentPress.com)
Cover photo by Brittany Moser (selfie) at Maroon Bells outside of Aspen, CO

ISBN: 978-1-7330864-0-0 (paperback)
ISBN: 978-1-7330864-1-7 (hardcover)

CONTENTS

FOREWORD

MY NAME IS **P**HILIP Moser, father of Brittany Moser. I was born in Angola, Indiana, on December 14, 1956. Angola is the county seat of Steuben County, Indiana and is located in the very north-eastern corner of the state. The county is known for its many lakes and is the home of Trine University. I have lived in Steuben County all of my life.

I was the youngest of four brothers, and all three of my older brothers died relatively young—the Moser family has experienced considerable tragedy. My father was a farmer, and I grew up helping on the farm. After graduating from Angola High School, I began working in different parts of the grocery business; and I still work there.

In 1978, I married my life's companion, Marilyn Jeanne Wells, and we have had two amazing daughters. The first was Marilyn Camille Moser. She was born on February 1, 1980; and we have always referred to her by her middle name, Camille. Camille married James "Mike" Schiffli on November 1, 2003; and they have two young sons, Mason and Tyson.

Our second daughter, Brittany Jeanne Moser, was born on July 27, 1984, and died unexpectedly on February 17, 2017, at the age of 32. Brittany and I formed a special bond early, but little did I realize how our lives would intertwine and how she would shape my later years. As our story unfolds, hopefully, the reader will understand how Brittany expanded my horizons and enriched all of those she encountered.

I am writing this book to tell our story, of how Brittany's short life truly made a difference to me and many others. She taught us:

- How precious the one life we have is and how we can affect the people around us.

- How keeping an open mind and a positive attitude can inspire us to do things we never thought possible.
- How to move out of what makes us comfortable and into a challenging existence which can turn every day into an exciting gift to be explored.
- How not to be controlled by fear, but to use our untouched abilities to seek unique, positive, and inspiring adventures we could never have imagined.
- To embrace change as a natural part of life. To enjoy every moment because there are no guarantees in this world.
- And finally, we won't be remembered by our things or our savings accounts, but how we made people feel when we interacted with them.

This is a story about the life of Brittany, our spirited, happy-go-lucky child who enjoyed every moment and has helped me to live my life to its fullest. She taught me how to laugh, to love, and to live in a way I never dreamed possible. This book is not about the grief of losing a child, but about making the most out of what we are given and living our lives positively and not out of fear. Brittany inspired me, an ordinary farm boy, to explore life, to climb mountains, and to write a book. Her story must be told. It's the just right thing to do.

Phil Moser
February 17, 2019

1

THE BEGINNING OF OUR LAST ADVENTURE

O N A CRISP, CLEAR late July morning in 2018, I set out on my final adventure inspired by my younger daughter Brittany. Eighteen months earlier, she had requested that she and I go to Sky Pond in the Rocky Mountain National Park. At the time, she was battling a rare disease; and just three weeks later, that disease took her from us. Now, I was fulfilling a commitment I had made to her. One of her last desires was to visit Sky Pond in the mountains of Colorado.

I was accompanied in this adventure by my older daughter Camille and her husband Mike. My wife Marilyn had decided to stay behind with Camille's two young sons because the ten-hour hike would be too long and dangerous for the boys. We were also joined by Crystal Nix Seeman, who was Brittany's cousin and a childhood best friend. Also joining us were Annika Fiedler and her fiancé Lars Berner, both from Hamburg, Germany. Annika had been our exchange student eighteen years earlier. After arriving at Glacier Gorge Trailhead in Rocky Mountain National Park, we were also joined by Casara Heaton, who had been a college roommate of Brittany. Casara had brought her fiancé David, her two sisters, a boyfriend, and her mother. Casara had been inspired by Brittany's enthusiasm for life. It had been over ten years since college, but Brittany had inspired Casara more than any of us had realized.

The sun had just risen above the Colorado forest to the east and at an altitude of 9200 feet, the temperature was in the upper 40's. We set out on an adventure that would test our physical and emotional endurance. We were all committed to seeing Brittany's request fulfilled, but there were many obstacles along our journey that would test us.

Upon arriving at the parking lot for the trail, we were met by Casara who introduced us to her family, and I felt an immediate connection. Casara had been touched by Brittany long ago during her college years, and yet that connection remained as fresh as if it had been yesterday. We were deeply moved by Brittany's friend

Casara and her family who had come so far and prepared so much to be with me on this special journey. We became instant friends and would support each other on this trek no matter what difficulties we might face. It helped me to be in the moment and enjoy the journey we were about to undertake and not to worry about reaching our destination.

After introductions, we put on our hiking gear; and a bystander took a group photo.

From left to right:
Lars Berner, Casara Heaton, Rachael Heaton, Kristina Heaton,
Katie Heaton, Wyatt Ford, Annika Fiedler, Mike Schiffli,
Camille Schiffli, Philip Moser, Crystal Nix Seeman, David Balicki

While everyone else's backpack was full of their hiking gear, I had something extremely precious in mine. It was a sealed container of Brittany's remains. I was taking her ashes to Sky Pond, the place where she, in her last request, had hoped to visit. This was the one place she wanted to go, no matter what. I had been planning and working towards this goal for a year and a half, and the day was finally here.

The day started beautifully. I awoke about 4:45 am. after a good night's sleep. Annika and Lars and I had gone on a hike up to Emerald Lake in Rocky Mountain National Park the day before, which helped me prepare for the much longer trek. I kind of wished Brittany had chosen Emerald Lake as her final destination, but she was a high achiever and never took the easiest route in anything. It only seemed fitting that she would challenge us to strive harder. Her insights were amazing, and she had done this kind of thing her entire life.

As the twelve of us began our four plus mile journey to Sky Pond, we were motivated by Brittany's desire to see this remote place and were also inspired by nature's amazing beauty. As we entered the forest, the smell of spruce and pine trees filled the air, and a rushing stream could be heard in the distance. It was just the inspiration we needed for a long and difficult hike.

About a half a mile into our hike, we arrived at Alberta Falls. The falls were more substantial because of recent heavy rains. We stopped for our first break, to take pictures and to enjoy the moment. Some of the guys had pictures taken of themselves uncomfortably close to the waterfall. Everyone else took pictures of themselves surrounded by the beautiful natural setting. We were now warm enough to take off our hiking jackets and reveal that seven of us were wearing the same shirt, a special design made especially for this trek to Sky Pond.

The sky blue t-shirts read "Fearless for Brittany" on the front with three stars at the end of her name representing the three star tattoos she had on her upper arm. The letter 'B' was turned sideways to look like a heart.

On the back was an Addison Disease awareness logo designed especially for her. It was in the shape of a butterfly with a listing of all the symptoms of Addison's on the inside of the wing's logo. Camille's workplace had designed the logo over a year before. It was beautifully done as a tribute to Brittany and to help bring awareness to this rare condition.

We then proceeded to our next destination, The Loch. The trail was becoming much more rugged and narrow. It was important to stay hydrated as the effects of the high altitude were beginning to be felt. It was also important to keep a steady pace and to watch our footing on every step, to avoid twisting an ankle or even fall. At one point, I retrieved a bottle of water out my backpack, readjusted my backpack, and the momentum of the added weight of the pack threw me off balance. I nearly fell over the edge of a cliff. I had not trained with this much added weight, and it took extra effort to keep a proper balance. I didn't let anyone know about the problem and tried to remain focused on reaching our destination.

The trail became steeper and even more dangerous, but the natural beauty was also more incredible. Brittany's spirit was with us. She loved taking pictures in natural settings, and we took a lot of them in her memory. After climbing a steep ascent, we arrived at The Loch, a beautiful subalpine lake surrounded by thinning spruces and jagged mountains. The peaceful waters made a perfect setting for more pictures and a rest stop before the next leg of our journey to Timberline Falls.

Continuing on the trail around The Loch, I caught a glimpse of Timberline Falls in the distance about one and a half miles away. The trail narrowed in places, and much of the time we were in single file. The temperature warmed, and I could feel the effects of the altitude and fatigue on my sixty-one-year-old body. But Brittany's spirit was alive in me. She had taught me to push myself past the barriers I put on myself if I truly wanted to achieve something.

Farther up the trail, the trees thinned as we were ascending above the spruce tree line. The views changed dramatically and revealed a magnificent waterfall. Ahead of us, before a steep and rocky ascent, was the bottom of Timberline Falls. At this point, I was extremely winded and needed to rest, but soon my adrenaline carried me up the steep and rocky trail to the falls.

It was here that I took a much-needed break and reflected on what had brought of us to this beautiful place. It was Brittany's spirit. As I was resting, I saw the younger members of our group on a snowbank left over from the previous winter. They were making snowballs and throwing them at each other. That moment took me back decades to a simpler time when Brittany threw different kinds of white balls.

2
THE EARLY YEARS

IN 1985, MARILYN AND I decided to raise our two daughters, Camille and Brittany, in Hamilton, Indiana, a small town of about 1500 residents in northeastern Indiana that features a large lake. The town literally comes alive every year when the weather warms and the summer residents breathe life into this quiet little town. For us, Hamilton seemed to be the perfect setting to teach our daughters small town values and the importance of good character. Hopefully, the experience would prepare them for the many struggles life could bring.

Our older daughter Camille was four and a half years older than Brittany. She loved art and spending time with her friends. She was more mature and required less of our attention. Brittany was very different. In some respects, she was like her mother. She was outgoing, friendly, and positive in her attitude. But she also displayed an adventurous spirit which was unlike any of us. As a father, I had made a promise to myself to be available to my kids whenever they needed.

This photo shows our family during this period: Marilyn, me, Camille, and Brittany.

Every spring in Hamilton, the winter's silence is broken by the sounds of bats hitting baseballs and softballs. Little League, with teams that included both boys and girls, was a major activity in the spring. I was told that girls just played back-up to the boys at that level, but Brittany proved that theory to be wrong. It was on the baseball diamond where Brittany's true character first came into focus. She played Little League for two years, and the team won the championship both years. In her second year, late in the championship game, she made a catch that preserved the win.

From Little League, it was on to the next level where girls played softball. In Brittany's first year with the Angels, the coaching positions had opened up. Our good friend and a neighbor Stan Henney accepted the coaching duties and asked me to be an assistant. I accepted, knowing that it would allow me to spend important time with Brittany.

Brittany was the smallest girl on the team, but she was not intimidated by the older and more experienced girls. Throughout her first year, she drew lots of walks because the pitchers had a hard time pitching so low. We had a mediocre season, but just missing the playoffs. The next year, was much better. We finished in second place during the regular season and nearly won the final game of the championship tournament.

Next year, Stan and I returned as coaches even though Stan's daughter was too old for the team. That turned out to be a very good year for the Angels; they won the regular season and then won the tournament with back-to-back, come-from-behind wins. This was Brittany's first major championship. I have many memories from this year, but it was the fourth year of softball that revealed Brittany's inner character.

New coach, Dale Rakestraw, and his daughter and pitcher, Cheyenne, had led the Angels to the top of the league for most of the season. Near the end of the season, Cheyenne developed a leg injury. Fourth-year player, Barbie Williams, took over as pitcher and developed an amazing fastball. Barbie pitched us into the play-offs with a number one seed. We only needed to win one game to put us into the championship double elimination final.

During the practice before the semifinal game, we learned that Barbie would not be able to pitch for several days due to an injury. This meant that we had no experienced pitchers for the tournament. Dale asked me, "Has Brittany ever pitched?"

I replied that she hadn't, that she was happy to play right field. Dale took Brittany to the sidelines and had her throw some pitches. Afterward, he asked me to practice pitching with her for the next two days to be ready for her pitching debut in the semifinals.

The day of the semifinal game came, and I was nervous enough for both of us, for the Angels season would rest on Brittany's shoulders. Her team was also nervous. Brittany's pitches were just plain slow, and her delivery was ugly. But somehow, she was able to get most of her pitches over the plate for strikes. The other team just didn't know how to hit these arching slow balls. Inning after inning went by with the opposing team unable to hit anything out of the infield. Our hitters backed up Brittany with a comfortable lead. Each inning that went by, our team's chemistry changed from nervousness to confidence in Brittany's ability to will her team to victory. Brittany pitched the entire game. She yielded a couple of runs, but the team won a stunning victory that sent us to the finals.

The finals were in four days, and Barbie would be given the okay to be able to pitch again. The opposing team had expected to see Barbie's fastballs and were prepared for her. Dale told me to keep practicing with Brittany pitching just in case she was needed.

Championship day arrived, and Barbie was ready to lead the Angels when Dale told me just before the beginning of the double-header that he was going to start Brittany as the pitcher. Brittany and I were as surprised as anyone at the decision. He had seen the team rally around Brittany's last game and liked the results. As in the previous game, Brittany's pitches weren't fast; but she somehow managed to get enough strikes to be very effective. Inning after inning, her confidence grew; and so did the support from her teammates and fans. Even Barbie loved seeing a good underdog story play out. Once again, the hitters could not connect with those looping rainbow pitches. Brittany pitched another complete game for a win leaving the Angels one win away from another championship.

Barbie would surely pitch the next game, and our chances for victory would also increase. However, Dale informed me between games that he planned for Brittany to start the second game. Brittany and I were stunned but realized he must have a good reason. As the second game began, Brittany continued to frustrate hitters with her off-speed pitches. I asked Dale, "How come they can't hit her pitching?"

He answered, "It's all about timing. They expected Barbie to pitch, and they practiced for four days getting ready to face fast pitches. They weren't expecting Brittany to pitch at all."

By the fourth inning, Brittany's luck had turned. She had walked the last two batters, and the bases were loaded bringing the tying run to the plate. Dale slowly walked to the mound and took the ball from Brittany and gave it to Barbie. A red-faced and exhausted Brittany returned to right field with the crowd on both sides of the field applauding her. She had given the performance of a lifetime, one that showed her true character and determination.

Seven strikeouts later, the championship belonged to the Angels. Just three games earlier, the fate of the Angels looked grim, but a happy-go-lucky kid had faced down her fears and found something inside that allowed her to embrace the uncomfortable and to move forward. There was a reason for celebration on many fronts.

After the presentation of trophies, Brittany ran over to me on the sidelines and handed me her trophy. "Dad, this is for you. You never got to play baseball when you were growing up because you and Uncle Doug had to take care of the farm, and I just wanted to thank you for spending so much time with me. I could not have done this without you."

I was completely shocked by this gesture. It showed me what a good, loving, and caring person she was, not just a champion, but one with a heart of gold. I felt a pride that does not come with a trophy. Brittany did not believe in no-win situations; she believed that with determination, she could transform almost any situation into a positive outcome.

3

HIGH SCHOOL YEARS

BRITTANY ENJOYED SCHOOL; AND by August of each year, she could hardly wait for school to begin. She welcomed a challenge and chose the academic honors curriculum to improve her chances of being accepted into a good university. As a freshman, she signed up for the most difficult classes available, but Hamilton High School offered few choices. Her graduating class only had 44 students. In addition to her academics, she was always involved in sports and kept Marilyn and me running with volleyball, basketball, softball, and even track her senior year.

In Brittany's sophomore year, a unique opportunity arose that would change our family's dynamics forever. Hamilton High School had accepted a foreign exchange student formally from nearby DeKalb High School. As a result of the transfer, the original host family had to transport Annika Fiedler twenty-five miles roundtrip to school twice a day. The time and cost had become a strain on the family's resources.

At that point, fate intervened. While Marilyn was talking to a customer at the store where she worked, the woman asked if we might consider hosting an exchange student. Marilyn and I had talked about hosting an exchange student but had not taken any action up to that point. A previous experience had occurred years earlier when we had hosted a student from England. She was part of a Girl Scouts' exchange program, and it had been a pleasant experience. Brittany had signed us up without asking us first.

We casually asked Brittany if she knew Annika from school, and she immediately lit up and said, "Yes, absolutely." She told us that Annika was a kind, shy, and thoughtful student from Hamburg, Germany. Based on her recommendation, we agreed to proceed; and the interview with Annika and her counselor went well. When Annika joined us, our family began a new chapter that opened our hearts and minds and broadened our perspective of the world.

Annika made friends easily. She was such a good listener and genuinely cared about people. She enjoyed learning about America, and we enjoyed learning about Germany. When the holidays came, our family get-togethers were extra special with Annika telling stories from her homeland and our accepting her as part of our family.

Brittany and Annika were an unlikely pair that fate would join, but the two became buddies right from the start. Brittany was fascinated by Annika's caring interest in her and her American lifestyle. Annika liked Brittany's wit, humor, and intellect. The two spent as much time together as they could. Brittany was often busy with school and athletics after school. Annika was also involved with the school and attended as many 'Youth for Understanding' functions as she could. The two kept Marilyn and me very busy; the school year went far too fast. We knew that our time with them together was limited, so we made the most of it. This photo shows Brittany and Annika at Annika's high school graduation.

When spring break came, we decided to take the girls to Disney World in Florida for a week. We stayed at one of the Disney resorts which allowed us more time in the parks. Even when we got soaked in the rain, we still laughed at each other. While there, we all bought rain ponchos that we have kept for memories. Back home, the school year passed quickly; and we knew it would soon be time for us to say goodbye to Annika. She would return to Hamburg at the end of the school year.

Marilyn and I both cried when Annika left, but Brittany was much more mature about Annika leaving. She remained upbeat knowing that this was not the end but the beginning of more adventures, and she was right. Annika had added so much to our family awareness of the world and opened our eyes to many things we had taken for granted.

During Brittany's senior year, we were able to support her academic and sports activities. In volleyball, she continued to excel and received the MVP award at the fall sports banquet. I congratulated her on her achievement, and she replied, "I could not have done it without you." It was an acknowledgment every parent wants to hear.

The year flew by with the academic and sports activities, but Brittany always kept her eye on the biggest prize, Academic Honors Diploma. This honor would assure her of getting into a good university and possibly earning a scholarship.

Times were changing in our family. Our older daughter Camille decided to settle down with her boyfriend of four years and married Mike Schiffli on November 1, 2003. Brittany had been accepted to Ball State University in Muncie, Indiana. She was excited because she had visited the campus and thought it would be a great place for her to accomplish her academic goals.

As the school year wound down, Marilyn and I were making preparations for a special graduation party for Brittany and to put all her achievements on display. She had accomplished so much.

Marilyn made posters of Brittany's achievements during every one of her twelve years in school. She loved to do this and is very good at it.

The invitations had been sent out, the food and cake ordered, and the decorations were ready to be hung.

The day before graduation, there was a practice scheduled for the ceremony. Brittany would have an opportunity to practice her opening ceremony speech. She had been asked to deliver the speech because she was the senior class secretary. She was also a bright, positive, and upbeat person who seemed to have everything going for her. She was the perfect choice to deliver the opening graduation speech.

When Brittany returned from graduation practice, she was in tears. What could have possibly gone wrong? She said that on the day of a special school trip to Indianapolis to see President George W. Bush, there had also been a final exam in one of her math classes that she had missed. As a result, she would receive a zero on her final. She was told that she would not receive academic honors and did not even have enough credits to graduate. In her mind, it meant that four years of hard work and possibly her future were gone.

The only option available to her was to study that night, take the test in the morning, have it graded, and then see if she would be eligible to graduate with academic honors. After calming her down, I told her to get her books out and I would help her. It was around 8 p.m. graduation eve. Most students were in early celebration mode, but not Brittany. We studied until 2 a.m. when we could no longer stay awake. The new day had arrived.

This graduation day would be unlike any that I had ever known. It could be a very good day or a really bad one. Brittany left for the graduation ceremony an hour before it was to start, not knowing her fate and whether her efforts were enough to achieve the goal she had worked four years to accomplish.

Marilyn and I arrived early for graduation and waited for some sign of how this event would unfold. I spotted Brittany down a narrow hallway filled with other graduates ready for the ceremony to begin. We made eye contact and she had the biggest smile I have ever seen. She nodded to signify she was an "academic honors" student. She had done it, with a little help from her dad.

Brittany went on to deliver a speech full of optimism and an underlying message that one should never give up or quit. In the packed gymnasium, no one would fully comprehend the true meaning of those words except Brittany, Marilyn, and me. One of her classmates later remembered a quote that Brittany had used:

"I'm good at being uncomfortable, so I keep changing all the time. I don't want to be content. I don't want to be complete. Deliver me, from being content and complete."

4

COLLEGE DAYS

As BRITTANY READIED HERSELF for college, I wondered if our relationship might have seen its best days; she was maturing and clearly becoming more independent. She had dreamed of the day when she would finally get to experience more of the world than a small town in northern Indiana could offer. She had made the most of her small town experience, making great friends and excelling in sports and academics. She had big ideas and loved people with views different from hers. She loved the exchange students she had met and had wanted to be one herself.

During her first year at Ball State University, Brittany was required to stay in a dorm room with another student. She was anxious about this, but also excited to meet her new roommate and for the opportunity to begin college life. As a parent, it was extremely difficult for me to say goodbye to a person I had spent so much time with. Mentally I knew that life is a process of letting go, but it just didn't seem fair.

Brittany was all smiles and tried to reassure Marilyn and me that everything would be okay. "It's okay, Mom and Dad. I still have your phone number if I need anything. Believe me when I say I will be just fine." Her positive outlook had proven to be right so many times in the past. Hopefully, this was just one more opportunity for her to grow.

Right from the start, Brittany made the most of her college experience. She made the Dean's list her first semester. I know she studied hard, but she always made time to socialize and make new friends. For me, the difference was that I was not able to meet these new friends. I would only hear about them through Brittany's phone calls or when we would visit her. I trusted her to make her own decisions, but I was still hoping to be part of it. In reality, we never really grew apart as I had originally feared. I was always there to listen to her about anything she wanted to share. I let her know that I would always be there if there was ever a problem.

Brittany came home for Camille's wedding on November 1,

2003. It was the first time that I thought that something might be wrong. Instead of gaining weight as many freshmen do, she had lost weight. To me, she looked unhealthily thin. Marilyn asked her about it and threatened to take her out of school and get help if she continued to lose weight. We monitored the situation closely and hoped it was just her way of dealing with all her life-changing events. She continued to go through cycles of weight loss and then gain some back. We eventually sent her to a doctor and discovered that she had a thyroid condition that was hereditary on Marilyn's side of the family. It could be helped with medicine.

Brittany tried the drugs and reported that the side effects were worse than the condition. She believed her condition might be helped by a healthy lifestyle and pursued ways to achieve that. Eventually, she had success, felt better, and embraced a naturally healthy lifestyle.

Brittany loved her college experience. She enjoyed a variety of subjects and had a difficult time selecting a major. In 2007, she finally decided on a video production major, but that would require a fifth year at Ball State. She now had a goal she wanted to achieve.

By the summer of 2007, Brittany had saved enough money to pursue an internship at Soma Productions in San Francisco, California, a company that specialized in making commercials. As a parent, I was concerned for her safety and wellbeing. San Francisco would be so much different than rural Indiana. She made arrangements with other interns to look out for each other. She assured us that everything would be okay.

Brittany enjoyed working at Soma and learned about video production and women's health because they were producing a local TV show dedicated to women's health issues. One day she went with the production crew to a video shoot of professional models that were modeling clothes. When she arrived, the production crew told her where the dressing rooms were and to be ready in half an hour. She explained that she wasn't one of the models and was there as an intern. They told her that she could be part of the shoot anyway and told her to get ready. Earlier in the year at Ball State, a fashion major had approached Brittany to be in a fashion show to model the clothes that students had designed and sewn. She accepted. Brittany's body language radiated confidence with her tall and slender build.

On the weekends while in California, she joined other interns in exploring various activities in the Bay area, including a Giants baseball game and a trip to Napa Valley. One weekend the interns went whitewater rafting, and Brittany conquered one of her greatest fears. She had considered sitting this event out. I think the idea of not being in control and of completely letting go was what scared her the most.

With encouragement from the other interns, she suited up, willing to face her fears. They showed her that it was really just water and motion and that her fears were holding her back from having the time of her life. Her decision to go on that trip had a lasting impact for her in dealing with situations where she had little control and needed to trust in people who had her best interests at heart. She later told me that day had changed her life for the better.

Brittany returned from San Francisco wiser and more confident. She had made some great friends on the other side of the continent and a promise of a new career at Soma when she graduated from Ball State. I loved hearing about all her activities and adventures and was glad to have helped support and encourage her interests. She knew that she could not have done it without our support.

In the fall of her senior year at Ball State, one of her requirements for a video production degree was to produce an actual documentary on a subject of her choice. Her professor suggested a project that the architect students were doing as part of a downtown revitalization project in Columbus, Indiana, and she accepted. She asked me if I would be her cameraman and travel to Columbus. I gladly accepted. It provided me with an opportunity to spend some quality time with her before she graduated.

We borrowed video equipment from the college and followed the architecture class around when they would give a presentation of their ideas to businesses and local officials. We did interviews with the class and the local businesses that were involved in the project. Brittany was the interviewer, and I operated the camera. She was a great interviewer. She was so good with people and her calm, positive demeanor helped people relax in front of the camera which brought out their best. I thought she could make a great news reporter someday. She edited the video after she returned to Ball State and received an 'A' for her efforts and a big thank you from the architecture class.

I loved being a part of Brittany's project. We were a team again, and we worked well together. Whatever the situation required, we would not have to struggle alone. We both knew we could count on each other. Whenever I was with her, she made me feel like I was the most important thing which made me actually feel important. Her confidence and optimism were contagious and rubbed off on everyone around her. She could lift the mood of people in a room just by walking into it.

Graduation day from college was much different than graduation from high school. There would be no extra drama about whether she would pass or not, and she didn't have to give a speech. Marilyn and I were the proudest parents on earth that day. Marilyn jokingly stated that she might not be able to get through the doorway because her head was swollen with so much pride. Brittany's accomplishments would surpass all of the family members' academic achievements in either Marilyn's or my family.

5

THE MOVE TO COLORADO

AFTER GRADUATION FROM COLLEGE, Brittany decided to get experience locally before traveling to California to compete for jobs in the highly competitive movie business. She continued to work two part-time jobs in Muncie until she could make the right connections. One of her professors had told her that success would mainly depend on the quality of the contacts she could make. She believed this because she had seen how good connections had already made a difference in her life.

The year was 2008, and the country had slipped into a great recession; the doors of opportunity were mostly closed. She received a couple of job offers, but she felt they weren't right for her, so she called Soma Productions to see if their offer was still good. They informed her that with the slow economy, they were planning to close down productions. As a result, Brittany decided to keep working her part-time jobs in Muncie until the job market improved. It would be two years before the right opportunity came, and Brittany made the most of that time by saving her money and making connections with people she met at Mancino's Pizza and at The Gap.

During this period, Brittany and I grew closer. She valued my experience of living through hard times and making good decisions. We learned to trust each other's judgments about what we thought would be best. During this time, she would tell me about her millennial generation's ideas about the future, and I would tell her about some of my baby boomer generations' struggles from the past. She called me her best ally. We bridged the generation gap fairly easily with mutual respect. Brittany did not have any serious relationships during this time she was focused on her career and where that might take her.

Brittany's big opportunity started when her best college friend Jenny told her about her experiences in Colorado. Jenny had lived in Denver before moving to Ball State and thought that Brittany would like Colorado. Jenny rented a room from Denise Greco, a woman in her fifties, divorced, and an empty nester. Brittany called Denise to see if she could rent her basement apartment. Since she was a friend of Jenny's, Denise said she could. In Colorado, Brittany would be able to transfer her job at The Gap to a location in Westminster, Colorado. She would also have many more opportunities in her field than in Muncie, Indiana. Not only did I give my blessings, but I agreed to help her move.

Moving day brought mixed emotions. On one hand, there was the excitement of taking a road trip with someone whom I cared so much for and enjoyed spending time with. But on the other hand, I knew I would be flying home by myself leaving Brittany halfway across the country. I wondered whether our relationship would be the same.

We packed her car with everything that would fit, leaving just enough room to see through the rearview mirror. The plan was to drive to Omaha the first day and onto Denver the second. I would help her move in, get acclimated, and then fly home. By 8:30 a.m. on moving day, we had said our goodbyes to Marilyn and were off on an unforgettable adventure. By 1 p.m. we had driven through Indiana and Illinois and were crossing the Mississippi River into Iowa.

Brittany had brought her camera and took pictures of whatever caught her eye. Little did I know that she was planning to make a video of our trip together starring me as the person that she looked up to the most. Later I realized that the video would also provide a window into her soul, a window that could see beauty, love, and inspiration in a way that was unique to her.

We arrived in Omaha, by early evening, stopping only for restroom breaks and gas. It was 96 degrees in Omaha and the next day was forecast to be even hotter. We decided to get an early start to beat the heat. Despite the heat, it was great being with Brittany again. She loved a good adventure and being a part of it made me feel special. We both enjoyed exploring new places. While she was in college, we had gone hiking together in southern Indiana just to get away and connect with nature.

We believed that the second day would be more enjoyable since we would reach our final destination. We got an early start and continued west across the great plains of Nebraska. As we drove, we talked about any subject that came to mind, the past and the future and everything in between.

By noon, we needed just one more stop for gas before the Colorado border. I pulled into a gas station in North Platte, Nebraska and noticed swarms of locusts on the side of the station. Brittany was afraid; she would not even get out of the car to use the restroom. "Just get gas and let's get out of here." I finished filling the tank and returned to the highway as fast as I could.

An hour later, we reached the Colorado state line, and Brittany's mood changed dramatically. We had made it to Colorado, and in three more hours we would arrive at our destination. This was our first trip for both of us to Colorado. As we drove westward, she became more jubilant.

I wanted to stop the first chance we had in Colorado but missed the ramp to the first welcome center. Fate would take us to a second welcome center area for a reason. The representative was extremely friendly and gave us very useful information about Colorado. As we were exiting the welcome center, I noticed something very unusual. It was a giant sculpture of a butterfly. The simple inscription read: "Metamorphosis." At that moment, I realized that was exactly what Brittany was going through: a caterpillar becoming a butterfly. Brittany's inner beauty was revealing itself as a necessary part of her evolution. She would fly away with beauty and grace never to return to her simpler beginning.

An hour later, we watched the majestic Rocky Mountains rise up as we approached Denver. It was the gateway to new possibilities. We arrived at Denise's house by late afternoon. She was a talkative and energetic middle-aged woman who had raised two

children who were now on their own. Being an empty nester, I felt she would enjoy Brittany's company. I could tell Brittany enjoyed Denise's energy and enthusiasm. Brittany had made a good decision and I was glad to have been there to support her along the way.

The next day, we got her established in the Denver area by changing her mailing address, opening a bank account, and visiting her new job at The Gap in Westminster. Denver was a whole new world to explore, and we both loved what we saw.

Colorado boasts about its 300 plus days of sunshine, more than either California or Florida. It is one of the healthiest states in the United States, partly because of the higher altitude and thinner air. One's body has to adjust to the thin air by speeding up metabolism to get the same amount of oxygen. It's like getting a mild workout without the exercise. It was particularly good for Brittany because she had low blood pressure, enjoyed the out-of-doors, and had already adopted a healthy diet and lifestyle. She loved that Colorado people also worked to be healthy and enjoyed nature and outdoor activities.

The next day was my last day before returning to Indiana, and Brittany and I did some sightseeing together. She brought her camera along to capture the highlights. The first place she wanted to visit was the Red Rocks Amphitheatre in the foothills outside of Denver. I had read and heard about this unique place and wanted to see it. The amphitheater is built into a space known as the Flatirons. It is a one-of-a-kind concert setting and must be experienced to fully appreciate.

The time eventually came for me to say goodbye. A part of me wanted to stay, not just to be closer to Brittany, but because I loved many of the same things about Colorado that she did. I had the time of my life bringing her to Colorado, and I was so proud of what she had become. She was now ready to spread her big beautiful wings and share her love and beauty with the world. She told me again the words that lifted my spirit. "I couldn't have done it without you."

With tears in my eyes, I left Brittany there to start a new life. I had to let her go.

6

LIVE LIFE TO THE FULLEST

DURING THE NEXT FEW years, Brittany grew and matured and experienced life in a way I did not realize was possible. In September 2010, she took her first major hike to see the fall colors of the famed Colorado aspens at Kenosha Pass, southwest of Denver.

As a budding photographer, she took dozens of pictures from every angle imaginable. She knew how to capture nature in all of its glory. I thought most of her pictures would make great calendar photos. She was inspired by nature, and I was inspired by the way she could capture it.

Brittany loved Colorado for its natural beauty and the Denver area for all its social life and career opportunities. Life was good, and her future looked bright. She expressed her optimism in a letter she wrote to her Uncle Doug.

Hey Aunt Debbie and Uncle Doug!

Just wanted to check in and see how you're doing. As you know, I made it to Colorado. Me and dad drove down, August 10th, stayed overnight in Omaha, Ne. then arrived in Westminster on the 11th. I can't believe that was almost 2 months ago, the time has gone by so fast! I'm staying in a house with Denise Greco and she has been absolutely awesome. She's a single mother, in her 50's, though you would think she was 30, very energetic, very fun and adventurous. She wears ME out! We get along really well and we have movie nights and shopping trips and like to bake new recipes. She helped me adjust and find my way around here.

For now, I'm only working at the GAP and it's only part-time so I've been actively looking for another part-time job or full-time to make enough money. Still haven't found one yet but I am getting a portfolio and website around too so that I can send it to photographers to hire me. It's taking me longer than I thought so I hope I can get that all worked out soon. I'm reeeally wanting to start working towards a career soon!

As for Colorado, I love it. The sun is out every single day and the air is fresh and clean. Everywhere you go, if it's to the mall, it's a Kodak moment. All of the roads are very hilly and scenic too and I love driving to work because of it. The mountains are great, although I've only gone hiking once so far. I went last weekend to Kenosha Pass and it was the time when the aspens are at their peak so they were vibrant and gold. I've never seen anything like it.

Denver and Boulder are both cool cities. Denver reminds me a little bit of Indy, but with more hippies and Boulder is full of college kids who all are fighting for some kind of cause. Animal Rights is a big thing here too and a lot of stores allow customers to bring in their dogs. Grocery stores even put water dishes out for them. There have been a lot of fires since I got here, and I'm sure you heard about the Boulder one that lasted a week. I saw big "clouds" in the sky right after it started and took a picture because I thought they looked interesting... then later that night, I saw the news and realized it was a fire. Oops.

This weekend, I'm going to Colorado Springs for Denise's daughter's wedding. It is at the Broadmoor, a very classy resort and it's supposed to be beautiful. I'll be taking tons of pictures I'm sure. Hope you guys are doing well, dad said it was pretty cold there lately and rainy. I hope it doesn't stay that way. I just came in from lying out on the deck, trying to get tan like everybody else here, ha-ha. Only in Colorado could you do that in October.

Take Care!

Love, Brit

In 2011, Denise told Brittany about a job opening for a videographer for Mares Productions in Denver. Brittany was excited about the opportunity and was hired. She would begin as an apprentice and after three months of training, she would receive regular compensation. Even though she had a video production degree, there was much to learn about the latest video production software. Mares Productions was a small local business specializing in weddings and other special events.

The videos she made were very professional and reflected how she looked at the world. Her videos captured the moment like nothing I had ever seen before. With each video, she got better and better. She went to new and sometimes exotic locations that I never knew existed. One place was the Broadmoor Hotel and Resort in Colorado Springs—a five-star resort catering to high-end clients from all parts of the United States.

I was happy and proud of her accomplishments and the way she had pursued her goals and dreams. She was finally using the degree she had spent so much time and energy to receive. She became good at video production, but she wanted more out of life. After a year and a half of video production, she knew this work would not be enough for her. She was an outgoing, very social person with an adventurous side.

During this time, she took on other part-time jobs to help support herself. In 2011, she worked evenings for Aramark Sports Entertainment which provided personal service for Denver's professional sports venues: the Colorado Rockies, Denver Broncos,

Denver Nuggets, and Colorado Avalanche. She moved up the ranks quickly with her experience and charm and was soon only working the VIP Suites. Earlier at Ball State, she had experience serving in the VIP Suites at Churchill Downs and the Kentucky Derby. She particularly liked the Colorado Rockies games because of her love of softball and baseball and the large number of games she could work.

One evening, she met Payton Manning, a sports legend she knew from Indiana. He visited her suite to see his friend Todd Helton who played first base for the Colorado Rockies. Brittany didn't get to serve him, but her coworker did and said he was a gentleman, and he left a $200 tip.

During this time, she was busy physically and also making new friends and connections. Whenever she had time, she would attend yoga classes. She loved yoga and had many more opportunities for classes in Colorado than in Indiana. She loved it so much that she decided to take yoga instruction classes and after four months of

training, became a certified yoga instructor in 2012. She believed in a healthy lifestyle and wanted to share everything that a positive, healthy lifestyle could bring.

Marilyn and I visited Brittany as often as we could, usually two to three times a year. We were happy to see her grow and develop in ways we could not have imagined. Yet we had the concerns that every parent might have for a single, twenty-something girl living by herself, 1200 miles away. She was adopting a carefree lifestyle of living in the moment and not worrying about tomorrow or even where her next meal would come from. I was concerned that this kind of lifestyle could not be maintained, and that disaster might lurk just around the corner. Brittany proved me wrong and always succeeded just when I thought she might fail.

When Marilyn and I would visit, we would visit nearby attractions and take Brittany with us. In the spring of 2011, we visited Boulder and Estes Park which is located just outside of Rocky Mountain National Park. Estes Park is a very unique tourist town that allows elk to wander freely through the town. Tourist and locals are amazed by these beautiful creatures, and so was Brittany.

After spotting a big beautiful buck near the famous Stanley Hotel, we stopped so Brittany could get a close-up photo of this magnificent beast. As she edged ever closer to get the perfect picture, a passerby yelled at Brittany to get away from this wild animal before it charged at Brittany for invading its space. Brittany got her perfect picture and risked her safety to get it. She believed that taking some risk to get the ultimate photo was worth it. She once wrote, "I carry an underwater camera in my glovebox just in case I crash my car into a river and at the last minute I see a kind of a fish that I have never seen before."

On that trip, we also visited the Gardens of the Gods Park outside of Colorado Springs. The Gardens of the Gods was designated a National Natural Landmark in 1971. The red rock formations were created during a geological upheaval along a natural fault line millions of years ago. It is Colorado's number one most visited tourist attraction.

We also visited Manitou Springs which lies at the base of Pikes Peak. Manitou Springs is known for its famous mineral springs. Manitou gets its name from Manitou, the healing spirit that the Native Americans believed was part of the area's abundant mineral springs. Brittany made a video of our adventures on that trip, and the video reflected how she viewed the world. She titled the video, "Life is short."

On another visit, the three of us went panning for gold at the Phoenix Gold Mine outside Idaho Springs. It boasts one of the largest veins of gold in the Rockies but is not mined commercially because of potential water contaminants to Clear Creek, which flows into Golden and eventually Denver. We didn't get any gold that day, but that didn't matter. I felt good doing something that I had never done before and sharing the experience with Brittany.

Brittany and I had developed a particularly close bond, one we were proud and happy to have. It always seemed to come so naturally. I remember many times when I would come home after a long day at work and wonder what Brittany was doing that day. Then, the phone would ring, and it was her wondering about my day. It happened on several occasions. It felt so natural and wonderful that our relationship was synced together even though we were in two completely different worlds 1200 miles apart.

In the fall of 2012, I decided I wanted to do a family vacation and rented a vacation home in Breckinridge, Colorado. With the family growing in different directions, I thought it was a good time to get everyone together in the heart of the Rocky Mountains Ski Country. I hoped that this famous ski resort town would provide a perfect setting for a much-needed vacation and time for everyone in our family to connect again.

From left to right:
Marilyn, Phil, Brittany, Mason Schiffli, Mike Schiffli,
Tyson Schiffli, Camille, Lars Berner, and Annika Fiedler

Camille and her husband Mike and their two sons, Mason and Tyson, would drive from Indiana to meet us there. Annika and Lars would come from Germany and meet us there after touring the Southeastern United States. Marilyn and I would fly to Denver and pick up Brittany before arriving in Breckenridge. Having all my family together again turned out to be a great experience.

On one of the days, we all went on an excursion to ride the famous Royal Gorge train through the bottom of the Royal Gorge. Passengers can sit inside in a dining car and see the gorge through the clear glass roof, or weather permitting, they can stand outside and see the gorge from an open train car. We spent most of our trip in the open car taking pictures of us together in a truly remarkable canyon. This photo shows the open car and the very narrow gorge.

The trip provided memories that I will always cherish. I strongly recommend this type of vacation for all families who can arrange it.

7
MY OTHER CAR IS A JET

LATE IN 2012, BRITTANY decided to take her career in a whole new direction. After making videos for nearly two years, she had accomplished her dream; and it was now time to nurture her adventurous side. I once heard a quote that says, "When you accomplish a dream, it dies."

Brittany heard that the airline industry was hiring flight attendants to meet the increasing demand for air travel. It didn't take long for Brittany to decide that this was something she wanted to do. One thing I knew was that when she decided to do something, her determination always made it happen.

Brittany had a job interview with United Airlines where she was competing with 100 other candidates for just two positions. She made it through three rounds of interviews, leaving only twelve candidates remaining. She thought her fourth and final round of interviews went well, but she did not get hired. United was looking for bilingual attendants who could speak Chinese or Japanese.

For her next interview, she flew to American Airlines headquarters in Dallas, Texas. She felt the interview went well, but she would have to wait a few days before she would be notified if she got the job. Back in Denver, SkyWest Airlines was holding a job fair for flight attendants, so she decided to interview with them while she waited to hear from American.

Her interview with SkyWest went really well and she was hired that day. She called to tell Marilyn and me the news and began preparations for her training in Salt Lake City. Two days later, American Airlines called and offered her a position but she had already decided to go with SkyWest. SkyWest is a small regional airline that flies out of regional airports in the western United States and also supplies personnel for United, American, and Delta regional flights. The company is based in St. George, Utah, with its training facilities in Salt Lake City.

Brittany's training began on March 20 and concluded on April 27 with no days off, not even for Easter. The first thing she learned was the importance of being on time. One of the trainees was dismissed the very first day of training because she was a few minutes late for class.

The training was serious and intense, but Brittany rose to the occasion as she had always done. She had to memorize the safety presentation used before each flight can take off. She learned the many safety procedures, most of which she hoped that she would never have to use. The lessons included how to put out a fire after a plane crash and how to perform a water evacuation. She learned that she would be the first line of defense in the case of a hijacking. Trainees were allowed to retake one test to help if they had an off day, but Brittany never had to use that option.

Brittany flew us out to Salt Lake City on April 27 without knowing if she would actually graduate that day because one of her final tests would be taken that same morning. We had been through this kind of drama before and felt that she would excel once more, and she did. This photo shows her when she received her wings.

Life changed for all of us that day. Being a flight attendant provided a unique set of rewards and challenges. On the plus side, she could fly around the country visiting all kinds of places and meeting all kinds of people. The same can be true for the negative side of being a flight attendant.

As a new flight attendant, she would be stationed at a domicile city [home base] in which her original flight left at the beginning of her work week. Attendants then fly to various destinations for four to five days until they return to their domicile city at the end of the workweek.

The rest of her graduating class were assigned to cities throughout the country, but Brittany was based in Salt Lake City. We only got to spend a few hours with Brittany that day. Her first flight was scheduled to leave Salt Lake City less than twenty-four hours after she received her wings. For Brittany, life became a whirlwind of adventure.

During her first few flights, she flew with her supervisor or senior attendant where she could be observed and corrected for any errors. She could still be dismissed if she made any major mistakes. Brittany did just fine; and after her first week of flying, she was on her own. She flew mostly in the western United States and Canada with many flights arriving or leaving from California.

I remember one time she called to say that she would be in the Midwest, flying to Ontario. I asked her, "Where at in Ontario?"

She replied, "I don't know. It just says Ontario."

I reminded her that Ontario is not a city but is a province in Canada.

After our conversation, she called me back ten minutes later, "I am so glad I talked to you because I would have told everybody on the plane that we were going to Canada." Ontario turned out to be an airport east of Los Angeles.

Brittany was living a lifestyle most of us would only dream about. She met new people every day including some VIPs. She traveled to new places that most people only read about or see on television, like Aspen, Jackson Hole, and Lake Tahoe. Through all of this, I was the person that she wanted to share her experiences. She would call me at the end of every work week to tell me about all of her new and exciting adventures.

There was one particular experience she couldn't wait to share with me. It occurred on a late afternoon flight from San Francisco to Vancouver, B.C. It had been a routine flight until she was summoned by the pilot to the cockpit door. That usually meant the pilot needed a drink. The pilot had already begun his initial descent to land the plane which meant that everyone was to be seated and prepared for landing. Brittany's original thought was that something was going wrong. She hurried to the cockpit door and knocked to let the pilot know she had arrived. The pilot opened the door and said, "Come in and shut the door. There is something I want you to see."

A very apprehensive Brittany did as the pilot instructed. The pilot continued, "As a pilot, we fly all over and see the earth in amazing ways; but I would have to say that this is probably the most beautiful setting that I have ever witnessed, and I wanted you to see it." It was Vancouver, at sunset.

The scene raised her heartbeat as she gazed out the windshield of the plane, Vancouver was beautiful with city lights that stretched from the ocean's edge to majestic snow-capped mountain peaks. The beauty literally took her breath away. She wrote us a postcard about the rest of her flight that day:

07/27/2013

Hey Mom and Dad,

Greetings from Vancouver! We woke up in San Francisco today, on my birthday. So, this will be the second time I've had a birthday in the "City by the Bay." We had a really nice hotel stay in Tucson yesterday and I got to lay by the pool under the palm trees for the majority of it. The Captain made an announcement to the passengers, so literally, every one of them [passengers] gave me a "Happy Birthday." It was really nice.

Love/Miss you,

Brittany

8
HASHIMOTO'S DISEASE

IN JUST A FEW short months, Brittany's life had been trans-
formed from a desk job editing videos to jet-setting around the
country, visiting exotic places, and meeting new people and VIP's.
It was a remarkable transformation; but as with every change, there
were a few downsides.

She was now living in Salt Lake City but kept her room in
Denver with the hope of being transferred back to Denver where
she wanted to live. Soon after she began flying, she put in a request
to be transferred; and after just two months a position opened, and
she took it. She called me about the news and asked me to help her
move back to Denver from Salt Lake. She would fly me from Fort
Wayne (FWA) to Detroit (DTW) and then catch a flight to Salt
Lake City (SLC). Because of a hailstorm in Detroit, I had to take a
later flight to SLC that didn't arrive until 1:00 a.m. in the morning.
We stayed at her apartment where I spent a couple of hours sleep-
ing on the couch. By 7:00 a.m., we had packed her car and were on
the road for our 550 mile trip back to Denver.

Brittany's home life changed because Denise had recently
become a new grandmother. She would be leaving Denver for New
York City where she could help with her new granddaughter so her
daughter could return to work as soon as possible. Brittany would
now be staying with Tim Gillette, Denise's friend and coworker,
who had an extra room at his condo. Tim lived near the Denver
Airport, which made commuting to the airport much shorter.

The dangers of flying became apparent the day Brittany called
from Portland just to say, "I am fine and don't freak out about the
breaking news headline."

I turned on the TV: Asian Airline Flight 214 had crashed on
approach to San Francisco International Airport and three passengers had died. Brittany told me that her flight from Portland to San
Francisco had been canceled because her flight was scheduled to use
the same runway as Flight 214. This experience reminded Brittany
that no matter how good life was, it could all change very quickly.

In August 2013, Brittany noticed that she had started to become nauseous on flights that had more air turbulence. She was hoping it was temporary, but it only got worse. She tried everything she could to help with nausea, but nothing seemed to help. When she finally got the time, she went to her doctor who gave her the bad news. She had developed a condition called Hashimoto's disease.

Mayo Clinic describes Hashimoto's disease as an autoimmune disease in which the thyroid gland is gradually destroyed. The disease, also known as Hashimoto's thyroiditis, is thought to be caused by a combination of genetic and environmental factors. It affects about five percent of the population. Early on, there may be no symptoms; but over time the thyroid may enlarge forming a painless goiter. Some people eventually develop additional complications. The condition was first described by a Japanese physician Hakoru Hashimoto in 1912.

For Brittany, the diagnosis was not devastating, even though it ended her flying career after just five months. She had been dealing with a thyroid condition for years. She learned all she could about her condition and double-downed her efforts to stay healthy. Since her condition might have been triggered by some kind of environmental factor, she learned everything about what might have triggered the disease. She explained to me how a physically active lifestyle improved a person's overall health. She attended yoga classes when she could and enjoyed the benefits that yoga brought. A positive mental outlook was also a major factor in her personal wellbeing.

Brittany's disease required her to leave flying; and she took a job at Sports Column, one of Denver's finest sports bars just down the street from Coors Field. It is the official sports bar of Coors Field. Brittany enjoyed working there and made many friends. She moved up the ranks quickly and soon was working the best shifts and meeting lots of people. She rented an apartment closer to her job at Sports Column. The apartment was located a half block from the state capitol building. She loved the location and the fact she finally had a place all to herself.

One day in December 2013, Brittany called me to tell me about a list of adventures that she had found on the internet. It was a Buzzfeed.com article titled "20 places in Colorado that will literally take your breath away."[1]

The Bucket List

Brittany Moser was sent this list by Buzzfeed entitled "20 Colorado places that will literally take your breath away." She and her father accomplished 13 of them before she passed away.

1. Crystal Lake
2. Red Rocks Amphitheatre
3. Royal Gorge Bridge
4. Bridal Veil Falls
5. Mesa Verde
6. Dinosaur National Monument
7. Horsetooth Reservoir
8. Chautauqua Park
9. Glenwood Hot Springs
10. Hanging Lake
11. Garden of the Gods
12. Devil's Head Fire Lookout
13. Rabbit Ears Pass
14. Lookout Mountain
15. Great Sand Dunes
16. The Purple Seats at Coors Field
17. The Sawtooth
18. Maroon Bells
19. Waterfall inside Casa Bonita
20. Trail Ridge Road

---

1   https://www.buzzfeed.com/geico/
    colorado-places-that-will-literally-take-your-breath-away

They were a combination of places and experiences so unique and beautiful that they could literally take your breath away. She wanted to tackle the whole list, to experience the same feeling she had had in the cockpit of the plane as they landed in Vancouver. She recognized that life is short, and we need to take time out for ourselves.

She wanted me to be the person to share the experiences with. Of all the people in her life, I was the one she could count on in good times and bad times. We had developed an undeniable bond, and I felt honored that she had chosen me to accompany her.

9

THE LIST

FOR THE NEXT TWO years, "The List" as we would call it, became our mission. There were all kinds of adventures on the list, but the one thing that they all had in common was that they all presented the natural wonder or beauty of the world. Some required strenuous hiking to remote places. Adopting the list came out of the joy of living, not out of fear and anxiety.

This is a photo from the Garden of the Gods.

One thing about "The List" that seemed like it was meant for us was the fact that we had already experienced five of the places, including the Red Rocks, Garden of the Gods, Royal Gorge, Coors Field, and the Trail Ridge Road. It only seemed fitting that we continue these adventures. The list felt like it was made just for us. From this point on, every trip we made to see Brittany included exploring places on the list.

In December 2013, Marilyn and I visited Brittany on our first winter trip to Colorado. Being from the upper Midwest, I was surprised by the mild conditions we experienced in Colorado with its plentiful sunshine.

Our first adventure was to go to Fort Collins to visit Horsetooth Reservoir, just a few miles west in the foothills. The Horsetooth Reservoir is a beautiful body of water that is a supplementary source of water for Fort Collins, Greely, and other communities in the region. It is most beautiful at sunrise or sunset. We took many pictures that day to capture the beauty of this manmade wonder.

On our trip back to Denver, we stopped in the city of Loveland. Loveland has more than 300 public works of art including 200 in bronze. One of the statues caught our attention and became an inspiration for Brittany and me. The inscription on the scroll read, "I am the master of my fate, the captain of my soul." The statue is a perfect example of how an unplanned experience can sometimes have the greatest impact. Brittany took several pictures and seemed to be emotionally moved.

Late that following spring, Brittany and I continued our adventures with Andy Wells, a good friend from high school days. Andy has had his share of struggles in life. He has dealt with a heart valve condition all his life and even lost a leg because of it. Brittany liked Andy's wit and humor as did Andy about Brittany.

The three of us attended a baseball game at Coors Field to watch the Dodgers battle the Rockies in a steady rain until the game was called off after six long innings. Even with the inclement weather, we still had a great time mostly because of Brittany's ability to be positive and uplifting even in harsh conditions. With our original baseball experience cut short, we decided to attend another game the very next day. The high altitude at Coors Field provides a unique experience for baseball fans unlike anywhere else. It is considered a hitter's ballpark because the thinner air allows the ball to travel farther with less resistance resulting in more hits and home runs. This photo shows us at the park.

The next day, the three of us visited another place on the list, The Waterfalls inside Casa Bonita. It is known for its unique entertainment which includes strolling mariachis, flame jugglers, and the famous 30 feet waterfall with cliff divers. Andy, Brittany, and I enjoyed a great lunch experience. We were among the very first patrons for lunch and were seated right next to the pool.

In September 2014, Brittany returned home to Hamilton for only the second time in four years for the wedding of Crystal Nix, a best friend and cousin from her early years. Brittany and Crystal had taken different paths in life since their high school days, but they shared a bond they would always cherish. On the way to the wedding reception, Brittany asked me, "What are you doing next week?" She wanted to know if I could fly back to Colorado with her to continue our list.

I'm not usually a person who does things on a spur of the moment, but this time it just seemed like the right thing to do. I realized how important the bond we shared was. I cleared my schedule and booked my flight without any second thoughts. It was a decision I will always cherish.

After arriving in Colorado, our goal was to visit four places on the list: Hanging Lake, Glenwood Hot Springs, Maroon Bells, and possibly Lookout Mountain. The goal wasn't to see how many places we could visit but to enjoy and experience these incredible places and most of all, to share the experiences together. After all, it was now "Our List."

As we arrived in Glenwood Canyon, a huge thunderstorm developed making the hike up the canyon too risky. We decided to attempt the hike on our return trip. With most of the day still ahead of us, we decided to drive to Aspen to catch a tour bus to see the Maroon Bells.

The mountains known as the Maroons Bells are located in the Maroon Bells Snowmass Wilderness of the White River National Forest. The two peaks are fourteeners, (14,000 feet or higher) and located twelve miles southwest of Aspen. Over 300,000 people visit the Bells every season. We arrived just in time to catch the tour bus headed for Maroon Lake. It is possible to drive to the Bells, but the tour bus provides the history of the Bells and we could enjoy all the incredible views along the way.

Once we arrived at Maroon Lake, Brittany and I found the beauty of this place to be absolutely stunning. Unlike any place I have ever visited, the sheer pristine natural beauty of this place was overwhelming. It was as if we had left earth behind and arrived in paradise. It seemed untouched by mankind, and we were the first people to discover it.

The Colorado aspens were in full color. The water was so clear that everything in the lake was visible, even the rainbow trout. We had arrived at the perfect time, and Brittany took so many phone pictures that her battery died. She borrowed my phone and continued taking pictures. I also remember how much Brittany enjoyed the quiet and calm of this place. We all search for this peacefulness, and we found it high on a beautiful mountain lake.

We spent the night in Glenwood Springs recalling the beauty of Maroon Lake and preparing for our next adventure. Glenwood Hot Springs is located between Aspen and Vail, Colorado, and is the site of the world's largest hot springs pool. The pool is kept at a comfortable 90-93 degrees, and the smaller therapy pool at about 104. Soaking in hot mineral water has many health benefits. The absorption of essential minerals gives the body a natural boost that is felt within minutes. We both found the springs to be an incredibly relaxing getaway, an experience everyone should have at least once in their life.

We left Glenwood Springs relaxed, refreshed, and renewed and drove back to Glenwood Canyon to attempt the hike up to Hanging Lake. Upon arriving, we found the parking lot completely full with signs that said we must exit if the parking lot was full. I also noticed that the clouds looked very threatening with severe thunderstorms headed in our direction. We decided to attempt this hike at another time. This was not a place I wanted to be in a thunderstorm.

We drove back to Denver, crossing the Continental Divide, and reached our final destination at Lookout Mountain. It is located 12 miles west of downtown Denver. The summit is famous as the gravesite of William Fredrick "Buffalo Bill" Cody and has several sites listed on the National Register of Historic Places.

As a thunderstorm moved through the area just north of us, Brittany pointed out a natural phenomenon that I didn't know even existed. Looking east over the Denver Metro area, there was a cloud that seemed to touch the ground with all the colors of the rainbow. Brittany said the phenomenon was called rainbow dust. There was no distinct shape to the colors like in a rainbow, but just a cluster of rainbow colors coming out of the clouds. I have always thought that rainbows were natural wonders and that good things were on the horizon. I had every reason to feel hopeful, especially after the incredible days that we had just experienced.

The next day we went on an adventure that wasn't on "Our List." It was late September, and the Colorado aspens were in full glorious color. Four years earlier Brittany's first hike was to see the Colorado aspens at their peak of fall colors on the Colorado National Trail starting at Kenosha Pass. The trail is located an hour or so southwest of Denver in the National Forest where the trailhead starts at an elevation of 10,000 feet. The aspens were in full color for us to enjoy. The colors were so bright and brilliant they almost didn't seem real. The bright Colorado sun lit up the landscape like a giant spotlight. I had never seen anything like it in Indiana.

We hiked two or three miles up to about 11,000 feet where there was a huge opening in the trees where we took some fantastic pictures. It was something I wasn't expecting to do, and once again I made the decision to follow my heart and instinct. Brittany encouraged these types of experiences, and we truly enjoyed our time together.

The following spring of 2014, Marilyn and I visited Brittany for two more adventures on our list. It was early April, and the weather was ideal. After a long winter, I was ready to get outside and reconnect with nature.

Our first adventure was to go hiking in Chautauqua Park located just outside Boulder, Colorado. The 151 miles of trails provide an opportunity to visit many diverse landscapes. Some of the trails lead to the top of the Flatiron Mountains which feature incredible views of the Boulder area. The beginning of our trail was very easy but soon became steeper and rockier. At about half a mile into our hike, we entered a pine forest which gave us cover from the bright Colorado sun.

After taking a break for water, we continued up the trail which became narrower, rockier, and steeper. We encountered a small clearing with numerous small rock formations, unlike anything we had ever seen before. The formations were very artistically created and I was told by a friend that it was most likely done by a religious group or organization, as an expression of gratitude. Each rock formation represents a specific attribute or event that person was grateful for.

Farther up the trail, the terrain became extremely rugged; but the views were increasingly spectacular. We were all getting pretty tired because none of us had trained for an exhausting hike like this. Brittany could go no further and wanted to start our descent.

For me, the views were wonderful, and there was no sense in over-doing it. We had achieved our objective and began the long descent back to our car. We also wanted to save some energy for the next day's hike up to Devil's Head Fire lookout tower.

Number twelve on our list of adventures was Devil's Head fire lookout located about an hour southwest of Denver. It is a "must do" hike into the area's only working fire lookout. The hike to the summit offers views of 100 miles in all directions. After leaving the main highway, we drove about eight miles up a dirt road just to get to the trailhead. I definitely wished we had had a four-wheel drive vehicle for this stretch of road because of large washouts and rough surface.

Unlike our previous hike, this journey began in a thickly wooded forest and was steep and narrow right from the start. The weather was sunny; but in the shade, it was quite cool; and we needed jackets when we were not in the sun. Some large snow-banks remained from the previous winter. This time of year, the temperature changes could be quite drastic depending on the exposure to the sun. Also unlike the day before, we took lots of breaks to rehydrate and refresh making the 1000 feet ascent very enjoyable and rewarding. We passed several hikers returning from the summit excited about their experience. They encouraged us to keep going because the effort would be well rewarded.

Higher up the trail, we passed through large snowdrifts that were protected from sunshine by trees. On the sunny side of the mountain, it was quite warm; and we had to adjust constantly to the ever-changing temperatures. At one stopping point, we rested and wondered if we had enough energy left to make it to the sum-mit, but we were all determined to press on.

I felt we were nearing the top when we reached a clearing in the trees and the terrain leveled out. Up ahead was a giant outcrop-ping of rocks with the fire lookout on top of the summit. A stairway of 143 steps would take us to the top for some breathtaking views.

As we reached the top, we saw snow-covered Pikes Peak straight ahead about 30 or 40 miles away. Every direction provided a different view. To the west were the high peaks of the Continental Divide, to the north was Denver and the foothills, to the east was the expansive Great Plains, and to the south was Pike's Peak. For all three of us, it was our first major mountain hike, and the view made it all worth it. We were all breathless in more ways than one. As we descended, we encouraged everyone we met that their efforts would be rewarded for reaching the summit.

Two months later in June 2015, I flew to Colorado so Brittany and I could continue our adventures. We returned to Glenwood Canyon to attempt the steep hike to Hanging Lake again. It was something I really wanted to do, but the conditions were not right for a safe and enjoyable hike. Once again, the parking lot was full, and we had to exit. We continued on to Glenwood Springs and relaxed in the hot springs pool for a second time and enjoyed the therapeutic waters.

The next day we traveled west to the town of Rifle, which was not on our list. Rifle is famous for two reasons. One is that the town has an open carry gun law that lets people carry their guns in their holsters like in the old west. A famous stopping place is the Shooters Grill where the waitresses carry revolvers on their hips. It is definitely unique and a great way to experience the old west.

Second, Rifle is known for its beautiful triple waterfall a few miles north of town. Brittany and I drove to Rifle State Park and had an easy quarter-mile hike to the falls. It was as if we had entered a Garden of Eden with lush green vegetation surrounding the tranquil waterfalls. The rains had been fairly heavy recently and created a stunning triple falls which visitors could walk under. It is a spectacular falls that few people know about.

I wanted to continue on that day to the other locations on our list, like Dinosaur National Monument, but Brittany did not feel well and wanted to return to Denver. Our time together was the most important factor in our adventures. As we were on no set schedule, we returned to Denver. Brittany was evolving once more, and little did I expect the chain of events that were about to unfold.

10

ADDISON'S DISEASE

O N OUR PREVIOUS TRIP two months earlier, Brittany told me that she had been seeing someone on a regular basis, and it was becoming a serious relationship. I was surprised by the news, but happy that she had found someone she wanted to share her life experiences besides me.

I had cherished our time and experiences together and wanted it to last as long as possible. But I realized that she was now thirty-one; and her biological clock was ticking. If she was going to have a family, she needed to start soon. I had seen how much she loved her nephews, Mason and Tyson, and she wanted this experience for herself. I had told her that I was willing to let go when she found someone who loved her as much as I did. She cried at the thought of that scenario. I believe she wanted me to be there like I had always been.

Brittany and John had gone to numerous places together they had even gone to Hanging Lake before I had a chance to go with her. It was still on "Our List" of adventures, and she wanted to go there with me. More concerning to me, her nausea had returned, much like it had when she was flying.

By August 2015, she was regularly sick and did not want to be alone. She stayed at John's apartment, hoping that she would regain her strength. She became increasingly sick, and eventually John took her to a hospital emergency room only to be sent home because of overcrowding. They were only accepting life-threatening emergencies. Brittany's condition continued to worsen, and she often couldn't work or even get out of bed. She lost weight because almost everything she ate often came back up. She called me one night, so weak that she couldn't get out of bed; and I told her that it was imperative that she get help. When I got off the phone, I told Marilyn how serious the situation was.

John again took her to an emergency room. This time he had to carry her. After some delay, not knowing what to do for her, the staff took her blood pressure and immediately admitted her to the hospital. They told John that it was the lowest blood pressure they had ever seen in a living person.

Before the hospital ran a test to determine the cause for Brittany's illness, she told them that she had been looking up her symptoms online, and she thought she had Addison's Disease. The hospital told her that they had never had a patient with this disease, but would take the tests necessary to see if that was her problem. A few days later, her doctor confirmed the diagnosis of Addison's Disease and that she had come close to dying. Marilyn and I cleared our schedules and booked a flight to be by her side. We needed to be there for her during this difficult time.

Mayo Clinic describes Addison's Disease as a disorder that occurs when the body produces insufficient amounts of certain hormones produced by the adrenal glands. With Addison's Disease, the adrenal glands produce too little cortisol and often insufficient levels of aldosterone as well. Approximately 1 in 100,000 people get Addison's Disease, mostly middle-aged women. The most famous person ever to get Addison's Disease was former President John F. Kennedy. Back in those days, the general public was not informed of this information because it could appear as a sign of weakness or vulnerability. While in the hospital, Brittany was given the steroids that her body lacked, and she quickly recovered.

Marilyn and I arrived the day she was released from the hospital. Our goal was to help her regain her strength and get her back on her feet again. When we first saw Brittany, we were shocked by her appearance for she was just a shell of her former self, just barely over 100 pounds. She was so thin that her bones were showing, and her skin was very much darker than normal. The good news was that her spirits were as upbeat and positive as ever. She viewed hardships as challenges that she could overcome to reach a better place. She had overcome many challenges, but this was the biggest one yet.

After helping her with the basic chores of cleaning, shopping, and laundry, we decided to get out and enjoy the warm late summer weather and go to Washington Park and visit its famous Nature and Science Museum. We wandered through the museum just to enjoy some time together be thankful that she had survived. We met John and thanked him for taking Brittany to the emergency room and for giving her the help and care that she had needed.

A big decision remained. What would the next chapter of her life be? Could she support herself and continue to live alone? How well could she manage her disease, or would the disease manage her? She would need time to recover and relax.

Brittany had to leave her job at Sports Column and find work that was less physical. Her legs and knees were weakened, and she could not do a job that required standing. She totally needed to rethink her career options considering her physical limitations. It could have been overwhelming, but she trusted that the right path would come to her like it always had before. She had substantial savings and did not need to rush to any decisions.

As far as her spirit was concerned, she was grounded more than ever. She loved the life that she had created, and nothing was going to take her positive spirit away. It was a choice that all of us have; but for her, it seemed to come naturally. Following is a quote that I think describes her very well. She kept it on her laptop.

"I am grounded.
My spirit is grounded deep in the earth.
I am calm, strong, centered, and peaceful.
I am able to let go of fear and
trust that I am eternally safe.
I am worthy of things Beautiful."

Carly Marie

During the next days, Brittany continued to regain her strength; and her blood pressure returned to a somewhat normal range for her. As a result, we returned to Indiana. Brittany remained in Denver and began her new life with her new challenges. She broke up with John as it became clear that they had different views on what each wanted from life. Her recent health emergencies had made it clear what her priorities were. The stress from the relationship was not something she needed.

Brittany had some difficulty with her medication; the steroids had dramatic side effects on her mood. She described it simply, "It turns you into a completely different person." She was happy with herself the way she was, and the steroids gave her petite body way too much energy and irritability. She would lose her patience, something that she highly valued. It made it impossible for her to enjoy the moment. She cut back on her steroids to help with the side effects. After a few months, she found a balance between the disease and the amount of steroids she could tolerate.

As the Christmas holiday approached, Brittany and I decided to do something special. We would both tell Marilyn that due to her illness, she would be unable to come back to Indiana for Christmas. She would secretly book a flight to travel home on Christmas Day and totally surprise Marilyn.

Christmas morning came; and I told Marilyn that for one of her gifts, we would need to travel to Auburn. She completely bought it; but as I drove past Auburn, she became very suspicious. I kept telling her it must be a little bit further. As I exited the highway that led to the Fort Wayne airport, Marilyn broke down in tears as she had figured out our surprise. A happy and grateful Brittany made our Christmas one we will always cherish.

The 2016 New Year brought an optimism that Brittany could manage her symptoms in a way that she could resume some of the activities that she enjoyed and find a job that was meaningful. As for "Our List," it would be on hold until she became stronger. We had now completed twelve of the twenty places on the list, and the hardest physical challenges remained.

During this period, Brittany became friends with Ricardo Narvais, a neighbor in her apartment complex. Ricardo had been in an automobile accident, years earlier, and his injuries had left him in a wheelchair. Ricardo was a spirited, uplifting person despite his setback and was encouraging for Brittany. He described her this way.

"She came into my life when I really needed a friend. And a better one I could not ask for. Her kindness, warm heart, and passion for life were impressive, considering what she was going through. I feel lucky to have known her."

Brittany believed in the body's natural ability to heal itself and tried many times to cut back on the steroids and let her body heal itself. She feared that the steroids were something she should not use long-term and that they were harmful. She did much research about her condition and tried many different approaches to managing her symptoms with diet, yoga, and detoxifiers.

Her research had concluded that something harmful in the environment had triggered her disease, and she was determined to figure it out. She had blood work done to determine if her body carried any abnormal toxins, and the results tested high for lead. Despite others' opinions, including mine, she had all the metal fillings from her teeth removed and replaced with nonmetallic fillings, thinking that it would give her some relief from her symptoms.

I had her see a therapist to help her deal with the events of that past year and give her guidance for the future. Brittany needed someone to talk to, and I couldn't be there all the time. I felt the stress; it was starting to take a toll on my own wellbeing. A normal week for me was to work my marketing job Monday through Friday and at the farm on Saturday. Something had to give. I sold the family farm where I had grown up. The farm had been in my family for sixty-two years, and I was the last remaining member of my family. I wanted the extra resources, but I mostly needed to lighten my burdens so I could be more available if Brittany needed me.

During April around Easter, Marilyn and I visited Britany to have some quality time together. Her spirits were good as always, and we had a very enjoyable visit. She even felt well enough for a short adventure. She had read about, and had always wanted to see, the famous Bishop Castle located an hour southwest of Pueblo, Colorado. The castle represents an amazing accomplishment of what one person with vision and determination can do over a long period of time.

Over the summer and into the fall of 2016, Brittany seemed to make progress with regaining her strength and managing her symptoms with occasional setbacks. At one point she had to be admitted to the hospital again because she discovered that her body could not break down potassium. Her potassium level was 8.0, a level that was so high and dangerous that she had almost died again.

Despite the setbacks, Brittany was determined to move forward and even took a vacation by herself. She just needed time away to reflect on her past and plan for the future. She had gone on other vacations to tropical locations in Maui and the Mexican Riviera, but always with someone. This time, she went to San Diego by herself to soak up the sun at the beach and to take a whale watching tour. She had been there before during her college years and thoroughly enjoyed scuba diving offshore and just hanging out at the beach.

Soon after returning from this trip, she got serious about the next chapter in her life and began searching for a job that she could handle with her limitations. She was a great interviewee and received offers for almost every job she applied for. After a couple of disappointments, she took a job at a company called Maximus that the federal government used to assist people in applying for health insurance and other government programs. The work would be meaningful for her as she now realized how important these programs could be. She began three weeks of training on December 1 and concluded just before Christmas.

Marilyn and I had planned to visit her in Denver just before the Christmas holidays; but this year, we could also help her study for her new job and career. I felt that it was important for her to support herself, or she would have to return to Indiana and stay with us. There were many times when Marilyn and I wanted her to come back to Indiana, but that would only make it easier for us, not for her. Throughout this period, one thing became clear to me. You can't ask a butterfly to return to its previous life. Once Brittany had enjoyed a life full of beauty and love, she would fight to keep it with all her strength.

I spent my 60th birthday in Denver helping her to study for her new career. Health insurance is complicated, and there were so many scenarios she would have to be prepared for when the time came. She was a good student, and there was little she couldn't learn when she put her mind to it. It was similar to the time we had studied together so she could get her academic honors diploma in high school. Brittany had a brilliant mind and a heart of gold and used it for making the world just a little bit better in a way that was uniquely hers.

At one point after studying for hours the many scenarios she might encounter in her new job, she got frustrated and had the most emotional outburst I have ever witnessed from her. With tears streaming down her face, she screamed, "Life sucks." It was a moment I can never forget. I had never heard this kind of outburst from her before. It just seemed to be getting worse.

I closed my book and went over next to her and listened to the pain that she was expressing. After thirty seconds or so, I said, "You're right, Brit. Life does suck sometimes, but you will always have me."

After a couple minutes, she collected herself and we continued to study. She had embarked on a new career path that she both needed and felt passionate about.

At this point and to make the situation worse, she realized that all her studying and effort might be futile with the election of Donald Trump. He had announced that his first order of business after he took office would be to repeal the Affordable Care Act (ACA). The position she was applying for was funded by the ACA to help people qualify for assistance to obtain health insurance. Since she hadn't worked for over a year, she was also receiving her own much-needed health insurance through the ACA.

After the weekend, Brittany took and passed a written test on the material that we had covered the previous days. I took that as a good sign that she had cleared an important hurdle that she had been dealing with. The following week, she passed all her tests and completed her training. It was a huge accomplishment considering half of the recruits that started the training had failed or dropped out.

During our visit, Marilyn and I helped her go shopping for clothes for her new job. She wanted to look professional and knew what a difference appearance can make. I also wanted to give her something for Christmas besides money. Marilyn and I noticed that she didn't have a sweeper for her apartment. She said she always borrowed one from her neighbor Ricardo. We found a nice cordless one and bought it for her. She initially resisted the idea, but quickly saw the advantages of having her own sweeper. I charged the batteries and swept her apartment for her only to notice that her hair had been falling out at an alarming rate. This was a symptom of Addison's disease. This photo was taken during one of our visits.

The new year, 2017, brought a sliver of hope that Brittany could begin a new career and be able to manage the symptoms of her disease. There were not many good options available for her, and this path needed to work; or she would have to come back to Indiana to live with us.

Her first couple of days at her new job, I would message her every day to see how she was getting along and to help however I could. She seemed pretty upbeat about the job itself but mentioned that all the other employees were treating the new recruits as if they were not going to be there for very long because Donald Trump had stated that his first order of business was to repeal the ACA. If that happened, the new recruits would be the first to be let go. Not only would she lose her job, but she would lose her own health insurance. It was an open enrollment period for the ACA and a stressful time to start a new career.

On January 14, 2017, she sent me a message that I viewed as a breakthrough. It read, "I have a place we need to add to our list. It's two hours from Denver called Sky Pond." Attached to the message was a picture of a beautiful mountain lake nestled between high Rocky Mountain peaks with snow in the crevices. To me, the message said she was back after months of tension and uncertainty. She wanted to resume our adventures by adding a new destination to our list. I enthusiastically endorsed the idea and told her we would do it sometime in July around her birthday. I immediately started researching the hike. Little did I know that a chain of events was about to begin that would change my life forever.

11

FREE AND FEARLESS

O N JANUARY 20, 2017, Donald Trump was inaugurated as our 45th President, and he announced his plan to repeal and replace the ACA. Although he was not able to repeal it on his first day in office, the reality was that the fate of Brittany's job and her health insurance were out of her control. There was little she could do about it. She continued down the path she had chosen and hoped for the best. She had overcome many obstacles in her life and this would be the biggest yet.

On Saturday, January 21, I turned on the news and saw the breaking coverage of The National Women's March across the country, and one of the biggest ones was in downtown Denver. I immediately called Brittany to tell her and find out what she knew because she lived just three blocks from the Civic Center where the march started.

It was late morning, and I woke her up. She told me that her job was stressful, and it was all she could do to get through the week. She would be so glad when open enrollment ended on January 31. She told me that she was spending her weekends just resting so she could be ready to start the next week.

I wanted to take her mind off her illness and told her about the Women's March in Denver and how huge it was. I asked her if she could see anything from her seventh-floor apartment. She said she couldn't but noticed all the parking spaces were full and there were people walking toward the Civic Center. She said she might go down and check it out when she felt rested. I also told her that she should do something she enjoyed on her weekends so she would have something to look forward to after a long week. I wanted to tell her what I had learned about the hike to Sky Pond but now didn't seem like the right time.

Brittany did go to the Civic Center that day and took some incredible pictures of people of all age groups expressing themselves. As a photographer, she could capture the human spirit in a way that truly expressed the emotion of the moment.

Brittany was a strong independent woman and supported women's causes whenever she could. There were an estimated one hundred thousand people in downtown Denver that day.

On January 28, I told Brittany that Marilyn and I would be going to Oscoda, Michigan, to visit Camille, Mike, and our grandsons, Mason and Tyson. Camille's birthday is on February 1. We had made this trip the previous four years that Camille and Mike had moved to northern Michigan. I sent her pictures of all the snow, and she replied that it was 50 degrees in Denver. I asked her how she was doing, and she answered, "Pretty good."

On February 4, I called to see how her week had gone and how she was feeling. She told me that she had made it through the week, and again she mentioned that she didn't feel that great. She was glad that open enrollment was over and things would be less stressful. We had a wonderful conversation that day about a whole host of subjects, basically whatever came to mind. We probably talked for an hour or so which is a lot for me. I didn't know what I could do for her except listen and try to encourage her in any way I could. She seemed to be on a roller coaster ride of feelings. Once again, I didn't mention Sky Pond and that it was considered a rugged hike. I knew she couldn't make it feeling the way she did now.

On February 5, she messaged me that it was Super Bowl Sunday. I told her that we were going to our good friends Ben and Sandy's to watch the game.

She replied, "Cool."

I asked, "Any plans?"

She replied, "Not really, but I'll probably go to downtown or the Sports Column or something."

After the Super Bowl, I messaged her, "Did you predict 34-28 Patriots?"

She replied "Yep."

The next day she messaged me,

"Dad, I forgot to tell you, but I LOOVVE my sweeper."

With a big smile on my face, I replied, "I am so glad. You make my day." Little did I know that this final act of gratitude would be the last communication I would ever receive from her. The next weekend, I felt a separation from her much like I had felt in the past, but I did not want to act on my worst fears. I still wanted to allow room for her to grow.

* * * * *

I sent a message to Brittany on Valentine's Day; expressing my love and after two days, I had not received any response. I tried to call and the phone rang, but she did not answer. This was not like her. I then called her landlord to check on Brittany. When she did, she found that Brittany had died several days before. Brittany died from what the coroner's report described as a full-blown, twin factor Addison's event. By twin factor, he meant that her Addison's had actually simultaneously triggered a secondary attack from her Hashimoto's disease.

After hearing the news, I felt my heart was literally ripped out of my chest. I wanted to die just like Rose on that chunk of debris in the movie "Titanic." But something deep down told me that I needed to go on and be there for the remaining members of my family. I needed to tell her story so others could be lifted up the way I had been for thirty-two years. She would want me to do that.

Marilyn and I grieved together briefly before we began notifying family members. I broke the news to Camille. Many questions remained, but one fact was clear. Since Brittany had never married, Marilyn and I would be in charge of her final affairs and arrangements.

I've heard it said that, if you lose your parents, you lose your past; if you lose your sibling, you lose your present; but if you lose a child, you lose your future. I had now lost all three. I needed to tap deep into the inner core of my character to find the strength to move forward. I couldn't help but think that somehow her passing was my fault because my primal instinct as a parent was to protect my children. I felt like I had failed at that. I believe that things happen for a reason, but how could I make any sense out of this? It just didn't seem right. The world must be upside down. It didn't seem real.

I believe that stress was a contributing factor that had led to Brittany's Addison's attack. She had been stressed about her new job, stressed about losing her health insurance, and stressed about her financial situation. Addison's had left her with virtually no defense mechanism to fight stress or any virus or infection. She had told us if she ever felt she was getting flulike systems, she would immediately go to an emergency room. Instead of protecting her body, her immune system, when experiencing stress or infection, would actually attack her instead of protecting her, making her situation much worse very fast.

Brittany was aware of her condition and aware of the fact that an attack from her immune system was a real possibility. She had nearly died twice before. She was determined to live the life she had built for herself, and she was not going to be defined as the girl with Addison's Disease. She would live her life to the fullest no matter what. It was the most inspiring thing I have ever seen.

As far as her final arrangements, I felt she should have the kind of service that she would want because quite frankly she deserved it. She wasn't an overly religious person even though she had attended many different religious services. She believed in being an example as a good person and practicing that every day. She expressed to me that being in the moment and extracting beauty from common things and being grateful were the keys to happiness and overcoming fear and anxiety.

Brittany broke the mold of everything that I had thought about being a good person and enjoying life. We had raised her in a small town with good morals and a good emotional foundation. She was capable of making her own choices and living with them. She would be accountable for her own actions. Nobody was going to bail her out but herself.

Even though she had never expressed exactly her final affairs, she had attended a celebration of life for a college friend who had died a year earlier and absolutely loved the idea of celebrating one's life instead of focusing on the loss of one's passing. If we think about it, it makes a lot of sense to focus on the positives of a person's life instead of the loss. We all have to die, but the way we have lived is how we can make a difference.

Marilyn and I quickly decided that she would not want us to be too sad, but to have a celebration. Our great times together with her far outweighed the feeling of loss that came with her passing. She had taught us the true meaning of life and how to live. That could never be taken away. The phrase, "It is better to love and have lost than to never have loved at all" couldn't be truer.

As for her body, it was about the only thing that really let her down. The last thing she would have wanted was to preserve her body and not her memory. We made the decision to have her body cremated. The coroner's office informed me that there would be a thorough autopsy performed to determine the exact cause of death to be sure there were no other contributing factors.

Marilyn and I had the unpleasant task of notifying family and friends of her death and telling them that her celebration of life would be in about a month or so. We also informed Annika and Lars in Germany about our plans just in case they wanted to come and be with us for Brittany's celebration of life. Having her cremated gave us the chance to bring her back to Indiana for her celebration and then take her to the one place she had specifically requested to go, Sky Pond.

The next order of business was to go to Denver and clean out her apartment, pick up her ashes, and bring everything home. As word spread about her passing, I received a message from Brittany's former landlord and friend Tim Gillette that we could stay at his condo with him and Donna, whom he recently had married. I took him up on his generous offer. Marilyn and I flew to Denver, rented a minivan to return home to Indiana when all our arrangements were completed. After all the enjoyable trips we had made to Colorado, this one was anything but enjoyable. It almost seemed surreal, like we were in the middle of a bad dream and couldn't wake up.

It took all our strength to finish this chapter in our lives. The help of our dear friends Tim and Donna Gillette made our burdens much easier. They gave us a beautiful relaxing place to stay helping us with everything including clearing out Brittany's apartment. We couldn't have done it without them. They even made sure we had plenty to eat.

Tim asked me if we had made any arrangements for a memorial in Denver because Brittany had made a lot of friends in the six and a half years she had lived in Colorado. Many would probably not be able to make the trip to Indiana. As I thought about what kind of memorial she would want in Colorado, the one place that quickly came to mind was the Sports Column, the one place that she had made the most friends.

I called Sports Column and spoke to Kyle and Ryan Cook, and they were more than willing to reserve an area for us to honor Brittany's life. Aaron Hyser, a friend of Brittany's from her college years and who now lived in Denver, Colorado, helped plan the event and notified all of Brittany's friends in the Denver area. Marilyn had wanted to do some kind of gathering of the friends Brittany had made in Colorado and this plan would work out well on such short notice. I was struggling to stay focused on what needed to be done and just trying to make some kind of sense out of the events of the previous few days.

On Sunday, Tim and Donna drove us downtown to Sports Column for an event that I never imagined I would ever have to attend. I was still hoping that Brittany would show up and this nightmare would be over. The people there were more gracious than I ever imagined, and I really felt the empathy. They even bought all the pizzas and drinks. They treated us like Brittany had worked there just yesterday. It had now been one and a half years since she had worked there. Marilyn and I met a lot of Brittany's Colorado friends and were moved by the sheer numbers of people that came on such short notice, but mostly, I was moved by the stories of her life that I never knew. I was amazed at how she had left such an impact on so many in such a short time. I was so proud of how she had led her life and even sadder that it had been cut so short. Even Denise Greko and the owners of the video production company were there, though it had been years since Brittany was in their lives.

At the end of the gathering, Marilyn had planned a balloon launch of thirty-two yellow balloons to honor each of Brittany's thirty-two years on earth. Each person got a balloon and a blank tag. Marilyn had them write a memory they had with Brittany and tied the tag to a balloon. We all went to the rooftop before I said a few words about how this signified our sending our love and being with her in spirit. On my word, we released all thirty-two balloons and watched them slowly drift upward over the Denver skyline. Then an amazing thing happened as they cleared the last rooftop. The balloons all made a southerly turn and headed straight for the sun, the Colorado sun that she loved so much. It was a sign; she was telling us she approved.

I went away from the event much happier than I thought I would. I had met dozens of strangers whom Brittany had touched. They wanted to express the joy of what she had given them. Marilyn was touched by how many grown men in their thirties sobbed sharing their stories about Brittany. The stories were incredible, and they treated Marilyn and me like VIP's for having raised such an incredible person. I slept better that night than I had in a week.

The next day we picked up Brittany's remains and headed for home, retracing the journey the two of us had made six and a half years earlier. We stopped at the metamorphosis statue in Sterling where I realized that Brittany was now undergoing a metamorphosis once again. It would be a spiritual life that lives on in the people that she had touched. Her life cycle on earth was now complete.

The next celebration would be in about three weeks, and Marilyn and I were already in full planning mode. We rented the second biggest reception hall in town, The Hamilton Life Center. It is owned and operated by the Hamilton Wesleyan Church. The gymnasium-sized building is used by the church for various Christian concerts and also for community events like this one. It would be the perfect setting for Brittany's Hamilton homecoming.

Two days before the big event, Annika and Lars flew in from Germany; and Mike and Camille and the boys drove from Oscoda, Michigan, to help with the final preparations for Brittany's celebration. I had gone through all the photo albums to collect pictures we would use to make five poster boards showing the various stages of Brittany's life. Marilyn, Crystal, and Annika arranged the pictures to tell a story of each period of her life. We set up the stage with memorabilia from her life that began in her early years and progressed to her time in Colorado.

By this time, we were receiving sympathy cards every day and had received some from all parts of the country and beyond. We had received so many cards. Because she had not lived in Hamilton for fourteen years, I wasn't sure that very many people would come to her celebration.

On the day of the celebration, Marilyn and I were at the end of the line to greet and welcome all the visitors; During the first few minutes, people trickled in and gave their condolences. As the minutes went by, the line grew longer and longer. Before long, the line extended far out into the parking lot. Nearly every teacher Brittany had in elementary and high school was there to tell me what a bright student she had been. People came from all over the country to be with us that day. They came from North Carolina, New York, Missouri, Minnesota, Washington, and everywhere in between. She had impacted more lives than I ever thought possible. I was so proud of her and sad at the same time.

I think Marilyn and I set the mood for the celebration as we tried to be strong and positive for our guests. We were sure that was what Brittany would have wanted. We had decorated everything with bright spring colors. Even the children seemed to have a good time.

After a couple of hours, we finally reached the end of the line of our visitors and it was now time for a reading from Jim Scott, a coworker of Marilyn's, who read us a book called THE NEXT PLACE. The book provides a different and positive spin about the afterlife that is easy to comprehend for all age groups.

After that, it was time to go outside and release the thirty-two balloons; with written notes attached from the guests. This time I was more prepared and wrote down some more of my feelings. It went like this:

"Brittany couldn't be with us today so we figured out a way we could be with her. By releasing these balloons we send our love to her. She showed us how to laugh, love, and live in a way that we have never seen before. For that, we are forever grateful!"

On my signal, we released the thirty-two balloons and they drifted higher and higher until they entered the clouds. Someone commented that even the rain was beautiful that day. The first warm spring rain had stopped just long enough for us to be able to send our balloons to the heavens.

The next day, as we were reminiscing about the events of the past day, Camille noticed something on Brittany's phone. It said, "Mom & Dad, if you find my phone please look in notes." Camille looked in notes and found these messages, the most powerful words I have ever read:

12

CONTINUING OUR QUEST

THE IMPACT OF BRITTANY'S last message was transformational, so much so that I could write another book about what a difference it has made in my life. But for now, I will only tell you about the immediate effects of that note and how it applies to this story.

My first reaction to Brittany's note was that she cared about our feelings, even if she should die. She was not planning to die because she had just started a new job and was continuing to live the life she had built for herself. But, she was prepared to die. She loved her life so much that she was willing to die for it.

The date was important because she had written the message on October 24, four months earlier. I had lost my parents and three brothers and never had the kind of closure that came with Brittany's note. In my mind, this was a "class act." Brittany was so thoughtful that she considered how her absence might affect those closest to her.

She is a testament to the power of the human spirit to overcome death and its darkness. Her spirit would live on in the people she had touched in her life. In the end, love truly does conquer all; and she wanted us to know that.

It is ironic that we had just celebrated her life in a way that she would have wanted, and her note was an affirmation. I felt good about the way all of us had honored her, and now I had proof. In all, we had received over 550 well wishes from people all over the country and Europe. Many were from people she had met and who had been touched by her infectious optimism and spirit. To me, there seemed to be one common theme of what made Brittany special. She showed people how to truly live in the moment. She uplifted others; and that action, in turn, lifted her. Following is a quote that she saved on her laptop:

*"There is nothing more rare, nor
more beautiful, than a woman being
unapologetically herself; comfortable in her
perfect imperfection. To me, that is the true
essence of beauty."*

Steve Maraboli

The note raised one important question for me. What about the earlier message she had sent me about going to Sky Pond? As I reread the message over and over, one phrase stood out for me "needed to add to our list." We had not worked on "Our List" for a year and a half, and it was so important to her that she still wanted to complete the list and then add one more destination. If she couldn't be there in body, she still wanted to complete the list in spirit with Sky Pond as the final destination. The list wasn't just a list, but a bucket list of adventures we could cherish forever. It was a no-brainer for me on what I needed to do next. We needed to finish the last eight items on the list with Sky Pond added as our final destination.

The hardest physical challenges on the list remained: Sawtooth Mountain, Hanging Lake, and Crystal Lake. For me to complete these challenges, I knew I would have to do months of physical training and planning to be able to complete these high altitude hikes. I would attempt them in late summer when there is little snow.

During my training, word spread about what I was about to do in Brittany's memory. Everyone that I told about my mission seemed to be extremely touched by the story and encouraged by my efforts. At first, I thought people would be saddened by Brittany's death, but then I realized that they were uplifted by the fact that I was keeping her spirit alive by doing this.

A couple of friends mentioned that it was an incredible story and I should consider telling the local newspaper in Hamilton about it. As the week of Father's Day approached, I thought that it might make a good Father's Day story, so I called the hometown (Hamilton) newspaper and left a message. After two days, I had not heard from them, (Hamilton) so I stopped at the local (Angola) newspaper. Ashlee loved the story and wanted to do a feature on Brittany and our adventures together. She created a frontpage feature titled "Final Adventures with Dad" which ran on Father's Day in three different newspapers in northeast Indiana.

Word spread about my story and what I was about to attempt. As a result, I had interviews with my hometown newspaper and radio station and with another of the region's most popular radio station. I also did a television news interview that aired on two of the most popular channels in northeast Indiana. Within a week, my story had been aired on two radio stations, two television channels, and was featured in five different newspapers. They were all interested in presenting my story about me completing our bucket list of adventures.

* * * * *

By July 2017, I had been training and planning for two and a half months and felt physically ready for the difficult hike to Crystal Lake, but I still wasn't sure what the effects of high altitude might bring. There just was no way of training for high altitudes in Hamilton.

I decided to do three of the challenges located at lower altitudes before attempting the hike to Crystal Lake. After arriving in Colorado, Marilyn, Camille, and I spent one night in Denver to share with Camille some of the places and memories that Brittany and I had shared. The next evening, we spent the night in Georgetown, about fifty miles west of Denver, to be ready the next morning for our first destination, Sawtooth Mountain.

Climbing Sawtooth Mountain, which connects Mt. Evans and Mt. Bierstadt, both over 14,000 feet, is recommended for professional climbers only. I asked a local professional hiker at the visitor's center if he had hiked to the summit, and he replied, "I've done all the hikes to all the summits."

He strongly recommended that we not attempt the climb—that it was too extreme. He told us that there were great views of Sawtooth Mountain from Guanella Pass, elevation 11,670 feet, which we could drive to. This was great advice, and we got incredible pictures of Sawtooth.

The next stop was to visit Rabbit Ears Pass near Steamboat Springs, Colorado. The summit has the shape of rabbit ears, which displays two large columns of basalt rock formations. One actually crosses the continental divide twice in a very short distance to get to the western side of the pass. The views going west into Steamboat Springs are incredible with many pull-offs to see the vistas.

Next, we traveled to Glenwood Canyon for my fifth attempt at hiking to Hanging Lake. Again the weather was threatening, but I was determined to make it to the top to see this natural phenomenon. Brittany and I had failed to make the hike to the top of the canyon on four other occasions because of severe thunderstorms and overcrowded conditions. But even with the threatening weather conditions, I was determined to complete this adventure. As we arrived at the trailhead, many hikers were leaving the area to avoid the potentially threatening weather conditions. I checked the weather radar on my cell phone to see the direction of the storms and it appeared that Glenwood Canyon would be spared the brunt of the storms and rains. However, the incoming clouds told another story. I decided to take a chance that the worst of the storms would go around the Canyon and our hike would be a safe one. If Brittany were here, it would be exactly what she would want to do.

The trail follows Dead Horse Creek, a tributary of the Colorado River, and ascends over 1000 feet in elevation for 1.6 miles to the lake. By the time Marilyn and I made it to Hanging Lake, the weather had cleared; and our efforts were worth seeing this spectacular place.

Brittany had been here earlier, and it was exactly how she had described it. The waterfalls into the lake create a peaceful serene setting that was absolutely stunning. The water is so clear that one could see everything in the lake including the fish. It was truly another example of natural wonder so beautiful that it would literally take your breath away. There was only one thing that could make this experience any better would be to have the person who told me about the place to be here with me. Yes, she was now with me in spirit.

The hike to Hanging Lake had been rigorous but nothing like the challenge Marilyn and I would have the very next day on our journey to Crystal Lake. Brittany's spirit was with me, and I felt that there was little that could stop me.

13

CRYSTAL LAKE

ON A BRILLIANT CRYSTAL clear Colorado morning, Marilyn and I set out on a hike that would test our physical, emotional, and mental resolve. The hike to Crystal Lake was number one on Brittany's Bucket List of adventures that she had asked me to do with her. This was the hardest physical challenge remaining from our list of adventures. I had trained for two months for this day. The time had finally come. I was concerned about my knee. It had swollen so much the week before that I had gone to the doctor. Our older daughter Camille had made the trip with us to Colorado; but was unable to make the strenuous hike because of her recent leg injury.

The planning was done. We had made the 1,250-mile trek to Breckinridge, Colorado knowing that we needed to adjust to the high altitude by staying in Denver (5,280), followed by Georgetown (8,500), and then Breckinridge (9,500). The backpack was filled with eight water bottles, coconut water, energy bars, and a can of oxygen just in case the air became too thin for my sixty-year-old body or for Marilyn. My shoes weren't just any shoes. They were hiking shoes that Brittany had purchased in Colorado and sent to me by mail for Christmas six years earlier. She said that I must bring them with me to Colorado and go hiking with her.

My concern about completing the task was that we might not be able to accomplish that task because of our aging bodies. This is something a person does in one's earlier years. With an elevation gain of 2,600 feet, this 8.5-mile hike up to 13,000 feet is considered difficult even for experienced hikers. We had made the hike to Hanging Lake the day before, but that is considered a moderate hike of 2.8 miles with an elevation change of 1,207 feet. This would be much more difficult.

We said our goodbyes to Camille and headed out on the trail. We planned to use our cell phones for pictures, communication, and a handy compass when needed; but we still wondered if we would really have phone service if there were a problem. With some uncertainty, we started down Spruce Creek Trail, hoping that we would find the trail to Crystal Lake. About a quarter mile down the trail, we saw the sign pointing to Crystal Lake. The trail looked very steep and rocky, but we were confident now that this was the right trail. The weather was perfect, but that could be deceiving because storms were predicted in the afternoon. We knew we had to complete the hike before the storms arrived.

About a mile into our hike, we heard rushing water in the distance which provided a background for our hike. As we hiked farther up the mountain, the sound of rushing water became louder. Before long, the creek was right next to the trail. This juncture provided the perfect setting for our first rest stop to catch our breath and take some pictures.

But why would a sixty-year-old man and his wife want to take on a challenge like this? Other friends I know were playing golf, spending time with grandchildren, winding down their careers, thinking about retirement, and planning for the golden years.

Love, Honor, and Respect: that's what had driven us to do this. I had shared these values with Brittany for thirty-two years. She had wanted to be here on this day, but a rare disease had taken her from us five months earlier. I was doing this because she would have done this for me because the father-daughter bond we shared could not be broken easily. It was just the right thing to do.

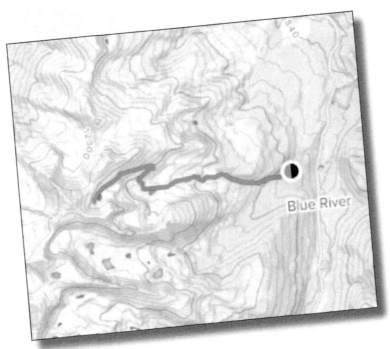

After resting and reflecting on our purpose, it was time to continue up the mountain. Crystal Lake was still miles up the trail. The trail was rocky and full of ruts, but we were surrounded by beautiful pine trees and the rush of a nearby mountain stream. We thought we were the only ones on the trail until we saw a young man, maybe twenty, jogging down the mountain.

It didn't take long until we were winded again; we were starting to get into thinner air. The babbling stream was getting closer and louder, and soon it was crossing over our trail. A half dozen rocks had been placed across the stream to help us cross the mountain stream. Six steps took us across and we were on the other side. We continued on for another mile or so when I noticed that the trees were thinning. We caught our first glimpse of the mountain peaks ahead, and Crystal Lake would lie at the base of those peaks.

Rest breaks were becoming more and more necessary and frequent. Our water supply was going fast. We knew we had to conserve our water as much as possible. The trail seemed to be getting even steeper or the air thinner or both. Farther up the trail was a ravine and another creek crossing, but this time it was much deeper and sharp rocks covered the creek bed. Marilyn went first and tried to stay on the highest rocks to prevent from getting wet feet, but was unsuccessful. I tried my best but almost completely lost my balance and also got my feet wet. The freezing water was the last thing we needed and an unexpected disaster. Once across, we both removed our socks so they could dry. After a few minutes, we put our shoes back on and continued.

After avoiding our near disaster, we continued onward and upward feeling the effects of our age and the thinning air. By this time, we were completely above the tree line and could see a plateau with a snow bank in the ravine ahead of us about a mile or so and possibly to be our destination, Crystal Lake.

The peace and calm of this picturesque view were broken by the sounds of three voices coming up the trail. We decided to wait and rest to let the three go past us. As they approached, we noticed three middle-aged women with all the hiking equipment needed for a hike like this. They were very talkative and friendly. Not too far behind them was a young couple with large backpacks. They all looked like they had done this before. As they approached, we told them to pass by us so we could rest before we continued. One of the women thanked us and said, "Where are you two from?"

I began telling our story of what had led us to this remote mountain and why we were doing this. The young couple arrived and began listening to the story of what had led us across the country to this remote alpine wonderland. I'm sure they could see that this wasn't something we did on a regular basis. All five listened intently until I had completed my story. They gasped when I told them Brittany had died. They sincerely wished us the best of luck on our trek.

Now the terrain was steeper and rockier. We were exhausted, but we knew Crystal Lake must lie just ahead because the trail was nearing the mountain peaks. A quarter of a mile or so ahead, the young couple had reached the top of the plateau and were admiring the view. Soon, the three women were doing the same thing. Could it be our destination? By then, our adrenaline had set in; and there was no stopping us until we reached that plateau.

Cresting the final ridge, Crystal Lake exposed itself to us in all its natural beauty. It's like an oasis is to a desert, a mountain lake is to a mountain. You have to take it all in truly to enjoy this magical natural wonder. I felt a rush like no other before. This doesn't happen like this back home. We had done it!

Then it hit me that there was someone who had wanted to see this but was not here. Brittany's adventurous spirit had led Marilyn and me to this magical place. I had now embraced her spirit as my own and now beginning to see the world the way she did.

14
FINISHING THE LIST

BRITTANY'S SPIRIT DEFINITELY WAS with Marilyn and me on our next trip to Colorado. We flew into Grand Junction, Colorado and drove to Dinosaur National Monument to see the incredible display of dinosaur bones encased in an environmentally controlled exhibit hall on a side of a mountain near Jensen, Utah. The exhibit hall preserves these fossils exactly where they were discovered decades ago. Seeing these ancient relics reminded me that our time here is short, and we need to make the most of our precious time here on earth.

However, it was the next destination that made our trip special. When we were checking into our hotel outside of Telluride, something happened that completely took us by surprise. I gave the hotel clerk my name, and she replied that we had been upgraded and that our entire bill had already been paid for. Three days earlier while waiting to board our plane to Grand Junction, a passenger had asked me about the reason for our visit to western Colorado. I initially replied that it was a long story and she might not want to hear all about it. Christine Odle pressed me for more details, so I told her the entire story about Brittany and our bucket list of adventures. She became a little emotional. She asked where we were going next and the place we were going to stay. I told her Dinosaur National Monument and Bridal Veil Falls outside of Telluride. She replied that she lived near Telluride; and if we have extra time, she would like to meet us for lunch.

Christine was so moved by my story that she paid for our entire hotel bill with the belief in paying it forward to people who deserve a break. Amy, the hotel clerk, asked me why a total stranger would pay our bill and wanted to know our story. I told Amy the entire story of Brittany and our bucket list of adventures and that we still wanted to complete them after her passing. She was moved to tears and said it was one of the best stories she had ever heard.

It was on our return trip from viewing the incredible frozen waterfalls high above Telluride that my cell phone rang. It was Amy back at our hotel to inform me that she had contacted the local news station in Grand Junction and told them about my story. She told me that they would contact me about doing a news story about our adventures in memory of Brittany. I did the interview the next day, and the story aired at three different times on two different networks. For me, the message is you never know when your life story can touch others and how a chance meeting can turn into something truly special.

In the spring of 2018, Marilyn and I returned to Colorado to finish the last two adventures on Brittany's and my list: Mesa Verde National Park and The Great Sand Dunes National Park.

Brittany's spirit was with Marilyn and me at Mesa Verde as we purchased the last two of three tickets left for the last guided tour of the day to Balcony House. This would have suited Brittany because she never liked to plan too far ahead and liked to let fate take its course. She lived in the moment as much as possible. We thoroughly enjoyed learning about an ancient civilization in the way that Brittany enjoyed learning about history and the wonders of mankind. Climbing 30 feet ladders to reach the cliff dwellings was a little dangerous, but added to the adventure and was well worth the effort.

The next and final adventure on our list would be to go sand surfing at the Great Sand Dunes National Park located in south-central Colorado. It only seemed fitting that this final adventure would turn out to be the most fun. Upon arriving at the dunes, we saw that the day would be hampered by extreme wind gusts of thirty-forty miles per hour which constantly shifted the sand on the massive 1000 feet dunes.

As we crested a large sand dune, we met a young couple returning from the higher dunes with sleds in hand. I asked if I could rent a sled for $5.00 for a ride down the nearest dune. I told them my story, and they let me use a sled at no charge.

They gave me instructions on how to ride the sled and use my arms for balance as I descended down the dune. Brittany's spirit was with me on that run down the dune. Failure was not an option. I had an incredible run, and Brittany would have been proud of me.

After the run, the couple told me how unlikely a successful trip down that sand dune was and that I got lucky. I had something else going for me more powerful than luck.

15

SKY POND AND BEYOND

I N THE FIRST CHAPTER, I told how a group of Brittany's family and friends had gathered to complete the last adventure that she and I had undertaken. After our group had rested, it was now time to complete the last leg of our adventure to Sky Pond. We had hiked past Alberta Falls and The Loch and were now at the base of Timberline Falls. Our party of twelve included Camille, her husband Mike, and friends of Brittany. In this photo, Camille and Mike celebrated.

I could feel the effects of the altitude and fatigue on my sixty-one-year-old body. Brittany's spirit was alive in me. She had taught me to push myself past the barriers I put on myself. After reflecting on the previous 32 years with Brittany, I was energized with newfound strength and determination to attempt to scale the most dangerous and difficult part of our hike: the fifty-foot wall of rocks directly next to Timberline Falls. Timberline Falls would be our last major obstacle to reaching Sky Pond.

I had watched some people returning from Sky Pond and saw how treacherous the climb would be. Luckily for us, David, one of the friends who had joined us, was an EMT and had lots of training in dangerous situations. He would position himself in the most difficult parts of the ascent and was there if anyone needed assistance. My backpack continued to be a problem, but that was not going to stop me from reaching the top of the waterfalls. I positioned each step carefully and made sure I kept proper balance and took one step at a time and slowly reached David in the most difficult parts of the ascent. He told me he was there if I needed him, but I thought of Brittany's determination to overcome the obstacles she faced. I reached deep within myself to find and overcome my fears. An adrenaline rush came over me, and I quickly and safely scaled the entire waterfall, not stopping until I reached the top. I rested and waited for everyone to join me.

One by one, everyone reached the summit and celebrated. We had done it! We had all reached down inside and accomplished something that we were not sure we could do. We were a unique group of individuals that risked everything to achieve something great.

Our reward was to enter a place that few get to experience. The area above the falls was a completely different environment, an open alpine region fully exposed to the elements. The wind was calm, and the silence made me feel like we were in a sacred place. We were on our own and all alone, out of reach from the rest of the world. There was no turning back now. For a moment I thought that we had entered a gateway to another dimension, and this was Brittany's way of joining us.

At this point, we used the cans of oxygen that we had brought to help catch our breath. We were at 10,800-foot elevation. The last leg of our journey would be to Sky Pond, and it was still over a half mile away.

The trail was extremely rocky and at times hard to follow since few reach this far in the hike. It was now near noon, and we had been climbing over five hours. Suddenly, the weather changed from bright brilliant sunshine to overcast with a darkening of the heavens.

We pushed on with a new sense of urgency as the weather conditions were deteriorating rapidly. We had come so far, and we were going to see this through. Brittany's spirit was now guiding us to our final destination.

As I reached the final ascent to Sky Pond, another adrenaline rush came over me much like the one I had experienced climbing Timberline Falls. Before us was Sky Pond in all of its magical splendor.

This photo of the whole group was taken to capture our achievement. (Photographer: Wyatt Ford)

This was the end of the road for us. We could go no farther. All around us were sheer rock peaks, much too steep to climb. Behind Sky Pond were the remains of last winter's snow that even July sunshine could not melt. We dropped our backpacks and enjoyed the beauty of this special place. I felt Brittany's presence as I absorbed this beautiful place much like I had whenever we connected. We had made it, and we now knew why Brittany had wanted to come here: to live fully in the moment and share it with others.

I looked around for a place to hold a ceremony to release Brittany's ashes back to earth so her spirit could be free. I found a flat boulder overlooking Sky Pond with the glaciers behind it. There was now a sense of urgency as the sky had darkened dramatically, and thunder could be heard in the distance. Camille joined me as I removed the sealed container from my backpack that held the remains of my once beautiful daughter. I broke the seal on the container and opened it to reveal Brittany's ashes.

As everyone gathered, I removed the ashes and began:

"On the way to Colorado, I began wondering if I was doing the right thing for Brittany and bringing all of us to this place. I was looking for a sign that all of this was okay with her. At that moment Marilyn handed me one of those chocolates with the little words of wisdom on the inside. I opened it and on the inside of the wrapper, it said: 'EVERYONE HAS A HAPPY ENDING. IF YOU ARE NOT HAPPY, IT'S NOT THE END.'

It was a sign from Brittany.

I continued . . .

"It only seems fitting that Brittany's earthly journey would end here in this place. A beautiful place for a beautiful person. Her earthly journey may end, but her spirit lives on in the lives she touched. We now carry her torch of optimism. We will never forget you."

With those words, I released Brittany's ashes back to the earth in the special place she had wanted to go with me. She wanted to be here no matter what. I had finally fulfilled her last request. Camille embraced me and let go of all her emotions. Everyone was moved by the chain of events, and Annika told me there was not one dry eye among us. I had continued to ask myself one question: Why Sky Pond? With the experience of visiting this magnificent place, I found my answer. This place was truly so very special, and so was she.

There was now a sense of urgency as the sky was now dark, and I began to feel sprinkles of rain. We needed to descend below the tree line in case of a lightning strike. We took a few more pictures, gathered our things, and started the return trip down the mountains. But as quickly as the clouds had gathered, the skies cleared to reveal brilliant sunshine again in minutes, as it had been earlier. It was as though the heavens were not angry and just needed to shed some tears.

We arrived back where we had started ten hours earlier, still absorbing all the events that had brought us to this special place, knowing that we were part of something much greater than any of us could truly understand.

* * * * *

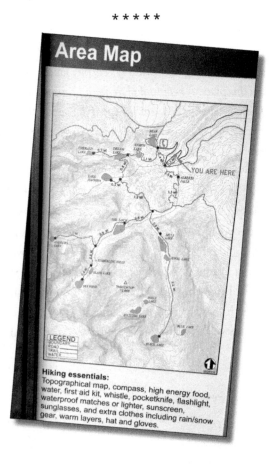

Hiking essentials:
Topographical map, compass, high energy food, water, first aid kit, whistle, pocketknife, flashlight, waterproof matches or lighter, sunscreen, sunglasses, and extra clothes including rain/snow gear, warm layers, hat and gloves.

Sometime after returning home to Indiana and reflecting upon all the events of the past year, something just did not seem right to me. We had carried out all of Brittany's final wishes and completed her bucket list, leaving her ashes at Sky Pond. It just seemed so final and empty. That's not how she would have wanted it. She was full of life and wanted to be remembered that way. She always encouraged others to take chances and be more alive. Two words in her final message stood out for me: "OUR LIST."

The meaning of her words came to me, and it was so brilliant. Once again, she knew more about me than I did. I had never made plans for my final resting place, because I always thought that I would figure it out someday. That someday had come; the place would be Emerald Lake.

Annika, Lars, and I hiked to Emerald Lake the day before going to Sky Pond. The stream that flows out of Emerald Lake connects with the stream that flows out of Sky Pond. Emerald Lake would be my final resting place and Brittany's spirit would wait for me until the time was right for our spirits to be together again for more adventures.

On my last visit with Brittany, I had made a promise that no matter what happened, she would always have me; and I meant it. We had a bond that could not be broken; not even death could separate us. I would be able to tell her about the last seven places on our list, and we could continue our adventures again. I am sure I am going to heaven; but before I go, I want to connect again with the one who showed me how to truly be alive.

* * * * *

I have learned many things from Brittany and how she lived her life. She taught me to find my adventure. Find your adventure in life, no matter how small. I am not saying you have to climb mountains or write a book. Just move out of what keeps you comfortable and into something that excites you. You will figure it out and be better for it. Life is a journey, so make it interesting by adding adventure to it. I have survived my loss by keeping my sense of adventure and I plan on keeping the adventures going as long as I can.

Grounded in gratitude and with a desire for adventure, I am now free and without fear and look forward to each and every day. Life is better than I ever thought it could be. I now have a self-love that is so great that I want to give it away just like someone did for me in back in Hamilton, Indiana, on a softball field, decades ago.

youtube.com/watch?v=eX3vRSbuRHg

I made this video to capture the highlights of our hike to Sky Pond.

I received technical support from ABC Channel WPTA 21 in Fort Wayne, Indiana. I also used the Apple Moments video program.

Filming was done by Lars Berner, Crystal Nix Seeman, and Wyatt Ford. I hope you are truly moved by watching it. The power of nature and human spirit to endure is truly amazing.

ACKNOWLEDGMENTS

MANY PEOPLE HAVE HELPED me in this process of reflecting, healing, and celebrating. My wife Marilyn and our daughter Camille have shared my journey and I could not have done it without them.

The following are a few of the hundreds who have supported our family:

Melane Wong (National Adrenal Disease Foundation)

Tim and Donna Gillette

Aaron Hyser

Brent Eads

John Cox

Danica Stengel

Hamilton Life Center

Eddie Bauer Outfitters

Apollo Design Technology

Christine Odle

Wayside Furniture

Ricardo and Patricia Rosas

Colorado Visitors Center

Miller's Markets

Smit-Ts

Kendallville Public Library (Rome City)

Tracie Schmidt

Brenda Maurer

Debbie Moser

Individuals who encouraged me to tell this story:

Camille Schiffli

Annika Fiedler

Lars Berner

Crystal Nix Seemen

Christine Odle

Pat Waters

Amy Sickels

Sandy Redden

Bob Howard

Dr. Lee Nagel

Jodi Strock NP

Ricardo Narvais

Ricardo Rosas

Renee and Tricia Nye

Danielle Pierce (Snooze Eatery)

Shely McGuire

Kathy Foster

Jane Scheiber

Sara Omlor (Manager at Eddie Bauer)

Linda Booher

Ben and Sandy Badders

Butler Public Library

Andy Wells

Brent Shaffer

Anna Allen

Zack Hahn

Mason and Tyson Schiffli

James Woosley

Robin (Georgetown Co.)

Jessica Ramirez

Newspaper:
Ashlee Hoos [KPC News]
https://www.kpcnews.com/features/life/kpcnews/
article_d39c6fc4-76b5-5542-a3ab-fca3f8c6cc30.html

Rachael Barry [Hamilton News]

Austin Candor and Teri Richardson [Fort Wayne Journal Gazette]
http://www.journalgazette.net/
features/20170808/unfinished-business

Radio:
Nichole Roberts [WMEE] 97.3 FM
Andy St. John [WLKI] 100.3 FM

Television:
WPTA 21, Fort Wayne, IN, Rex Smith, Free and Fearless:
https://www.facebook.com/watch/?v=743803945959973

WKJG channel 33, Fort Wayne, IN

KCCO 11, Grand Junction CO

KJCT 8, Grand Junction, CO

Those who helped with writing and editing this book:
Marilyn Moser
Sandra Redden
Dale Dailey

NADF
National Adrenal Diseases Foundation

The National Adrenal Diseases Foundation (NADF) is a not-for-profit organization dedicated to providing support, information and education to individuals having adrenal insufficiency, such as Addison's disease, as well as other diseases of the adrenal glands.

NADF informs, educates, and supports those with adrenal disease and their families to improve their quality of life. Their goals are to stop death from undiagnosed adrenal insufficiency; improve life quality of those who suffer from adrenal disease and promote the study of adrenal disease to improve treatment and find cures. NADF sponsors support groups across the U.S. in addition to several virtual specialty groups like inspire.com. These groups provide an opportunity to connect patients, families, friends and caregivers for support and inspiration.

Anyone wishing obtain important 'Tools for Life' resources or participate in a support group can find NADF at:

nadf.us

To help bring awareness to Addison's Disease,
this logo was designed specifically for Brittany Moser
by the staff at Apollo Design Technology in
Fort Wayne, Indiana. It is now recognized
around the United States.

A portion of the proceeds from each
sale of this book will be donated to the
National Adrenal Disease Foundation (NADF)
to help support those with Addison's Disease.

Made in the USA
Middletown, DE
03 February 2022

59581910R00089